DELANO

T0367234

DELANO

The Story of the California Grape Strike

JOHN GREGORY DUNNE

Foreword by Ilan Stavans

UNIVERSITY OF CALIFORNIA PRESS
Berkeley   Los Angeles

University of California Press, one of the most distinguished
university presses in the United States, enriches lives around the
world by advancing scholarship in the humanities, social sciences,
and natural sciences. Its activities are supported by the UC Press
Foundation and by philanthropic contributions from individuals
and institutions. For more information, visit www.ucpress.edu.

University of California Press
Berkeley and Los Angeles, California

Photographs by Ted Streshinsky

Library of Congress Cataloging-in-Publication Data

Dunne, John Gregory, 1932–2003.
    Delano : The story of the California grape strike / John Gregory Dunne ;
photographs by Ted Streshinsky ; [foreword by Ilan Stavans].
        p.   cm.
    Reprint of the Rev. and updated ed. published in 1971 by Farrar, Straus &
Giroux.
    Includes bibliographical references and index.
    ISBN 978-0-520-25433-6 (pbk. : alk. paper)
    1. Grape Strike, Calif., 1965–1970.   2. Chavez, Cesar, 1927–
I. Streshinsky, Ted.   II. Title.

HD5325.A29D8   2008
331.89′28348097948—dc22   2007021321

Manufactured in the United States of America

17   16   15   14   13   12   11   10   09   08
10   9   8   7   6   5   4   3   2   1

This book is printed on New Leaf EcoBook 50, a 100% recycled fiber
of which 50% is de-inked post-consumer waste, processed chlorine-free.
EcoBook 50 is acid-free and meets the minimum requirements of
ANSI/ASTM D5634-01 (Permanence of Paper).

For Harriet Harrison Burns

ACKNOWLEDGMENTS

I am indebted to Carey McWilliams, from whose many books about California much of the historical information in Chapter Four was drawn. I also would like to thank Cesar Chavez, Eugene Nelson, and *Ramparts* Magazine for allowing me to quote, in Chapter Six, from a series of long taped interviews in which Mr. Chavez reminisces about his youth and early social work. I am also grateful to the editors of *The Saturday Evening Post,* who published a part of this book in a slightly different form, under the title *Strike,* for their encouragement through the duration of this project. Finally, I would like especially to thank Ted Streshinsky, who was there during the long days and nights, and last, but most of all, Joan Didion, who has been there for five generations.

FOREWORD TO THE 2008 EDITION

Forty years after its original publication, *Delano: The Story of the California Grape Strike* retains not only its freshness but its urgency too. John Gregory Dunne's book centers on a five-year strike, organized in 1965 by Cesar Chavez and the National Farm Workers Association (NFWA), that in retrospect stands as one of the most acrimonious in American labor history. It catapulted Chavez onto the national stage, opposed a marginalized, largely undocumented minority against grape vineyard growers in the Great Central Valley of California, especially the town of Delano, and revitalized the base of several prominent political figures, including Robert Kennedy. At a time when the struggle for civil rights was defining a young generation of Americans, the strike—in Spanish, *la huelga*—placed Mexican-Americans on the nation's radar. It legitimized the grass-roots inspiration of the Chicano movement and might be seen as an early sign of the United States recognizing itself as demographically diverse.

Thus, given the historical benchmark that the Delano strike became in history books and the number of journalists on the scene, it is surprising that few eyewitness accounts of the upheaval are available. As the unrest moved toward its third year, Dunne believed that the strike was "mired in quicksand." Yet the amount of media interest was immense. The grape boycott orchestrated by the Farm Workers worked on a number of levels because radio, TV, and newspapers kept the clash alive while generating halfhearted sympathy toward the strikers among consumers nationwide. I say *halfhearted* because average Americans didn't quite embrace the full extent of NFWA's demands. They did refuse to buy grapes in major stores, and marches were organized in large urban centers. But for most Americans the strike unfolded as a distant event reported on prime-time news, one of hundreds that inundate the general public on a regular basis. To this day the agitation hardly raises an eyebrow among the general public. It hasn't made it to the elementary school curriculum.

Maybe it shouldn't surprise anyone that little reportage of lasting value about the event has survived. There are several accounts addressing the demonstrations of Chicanos in the Southwest at the end of the 1960s and in the early 1970s, and there is a collective biography of *la causa* by Jacques Levy, a mosaic-like recreation of the Mexican-American leaders and their odyssey. And Peter Matthiessen's *Sal Si Puedes*, released in 1969, is equally extraordinary, although it focuses more on Chavez as a man. But Delano is only a passing chapter in these works. In comparison, Dunne's volume stands as the single most authoritative chronicle of *la huelga* in the Valley— indeed, when a slightly different version of it was first published in the *Saturday Evening Post*, it was called "The Strike." It is also an eminently readable record of the factors behind the labor confrontation, the negotiations that went on to resolve the dispute around grapes and what was then known as "agribusiness," and the magnetic but radicalizing personality of Chavez, which evolved as the process moved along. It's as if John Steinbeck's *The Grapes of Wrath* had been reimagined in the 1960s and rendered into fractured Spanish. The *New York Times* said: "John Gregory Dunne's book is an exceptionally incisive report on the anatomy of the strike; a colorful, perceptive examination of its impact on the community; and an analysis of actions of both employers and labor so realistic as to make it important reading for current students of economics and public policy." And the *San Francisco Chronicle* described it as "a sensitive rendering of the atmosphere that permeates the great battle of Delano."

The book is an anomaly for other reasons. Its author wasn't known then as a left-leaning reporter of working-class protests, nor would he eventually make a reputation as such. Responsible for a dozen screenplays—including *True Confessions* and *Up Close and Personal,* coauthored with his wife, Joan Didion—and books like *Dutch Shea, Jr.* and *Playland,* Dunne is famous for his Hollywood inside stories and his essays on culture in the *New York Review of Books.* His lifelong interest, as discussed by George Plimpton in a *Paris Review* interview of 1996, was in describing "extraordinary grotesqueries—nutty nuns, midgets, whores of the most breathtaking abilities and appetites," which Dunne explained as a perverse fascination of a lapsed Catholic, adding that "the nuns and the monks were far more valuable to me than my four years at Princeton." Dead in 2003 at the age of seventy-one (his death and the illness of his daughter Quintana Roo are the topic of Didion's prizewinning memoir *The Year of Magical Thinking*), he was of Irish descent, a native of Hartford, Connecticut, who, soon after college, got a job at *Time* magazine, where he wrote on a variety of issues, especially for the foreign news section. Soon after leaving *Time,* he convinced the editors of the *Saturday Evening Post,* then an in-depth weekly to which Didion also contributed, to assign him to the Mexican strike in the Valley. In any case, he was amazingly patient in his pursuit of every detail about the NFWA, its demands, its impending impact on the country's future. (In the same *Paris Review* interview, Dunne argues that "writing is a sort of manual labor of the mind.") This was the first and, as it happens, the only time Dunne would focus his considerable talent as a literary observer of the labor-force revolution shaking America in the Vietnam years. The result is a strikingly balanced picture of the animosity that prevailed in Delano and an invaluable document allowing us to appreciate the volatile atmosphere at the time.

A lucid, intelligent, clear-headed stylist, in *Delano* Dunne has the unmistakable viewpoint of an outsider. His first paragraph places us on Highway 99, the road that takes him from Los Angeles to Delano. His exploration of the places he visits is multilayered. Eventually he zooms in on the agricultural past of the Valley, its changing population since the Gold Rush, the importance of the grape industry, the technological tools used in it, and the presence of Mexican migrants. He settles on Chavez as his protagonist surrounded by a galaxy of supporting characters. Neutrality is the keyword: Dunne's objective is to deliver a nuanced narrative summary of events without endorsing any one ideological stand. The impartiality works well, even if at times one gets the impression that the conflict he's exploring doesn't concern him fully, that it's only remotely linked to his own vision of the nation's future. Is this because Dunne was a northeasterner with a different sense of the country's social texture? His freelance effort would serve as his introduction to California, although in the end he would be drawn to the state by the rich and famous in Hollywood and not the beaten and downtrodden in the San Joaquin Valley.

There is a quasi-scientific aspect to Dunne's evaluation. He reflects, with astounding fidelity, on the labor debacle, allowing his curiosity to go as far as possible, at one point even applauding the grape boycott, but remaining reluctant to be swept away by the charisma and energy of the underdog. The approach does create complications and might be said to be inadvertently lopsided. I'm struck, for instance, at how the Mexican *huelguistas* are portrayed in *Delano* as a group in need of representation, mistreated, voiceless; yet their viewpoints aren't personalized. Prominent growers, teamsters, politicians, even religious leaders, are identified by name. The NFWA, instead, is an acronym. Dunne doesn't side with them; he just isn't ready to compromise his own emotions and loyalties. Still, at the core of his book is Cesar Chavez, whose mission seems to make Dunne skeptical, even uncomfortable. (Chavez is said to belong to that "inarticulate subculture of farm workers upon whom the Valley depends but whose existence does not impinge heavily on the Valley consciousness.") In *Delano*, Dunne tells a story that perfectly illustrates his reluctance to judge. When he returned to the Central Valley years after having finished his story, he tells us, a highway patrolman stopped him for driving too fast. "You were going 85 mph in a 70 mph zone," the officer tells him. After requesting Dunne's driver's license, the patrolman asks about Dunne's occupation and Dunne answers him. "Do you know about this grape strike here? That's a good story," the patrolman says. Dunne replies that he's been writing about it for a magazine. "Is that a liberal magazine or a conservative magazine?" asks the patrolman. Dunne answers, "They let you think pretty much what you want." The patrolman continues:

"You ever met this Cesar Chavez?"
"Yes."
He was closing his summons book. "He a Communist?"

"No."

The youth was silent for a moment. Then he unbuttoned his shirt flap and took out his pen. He reopened his summons book. "You were doing 85 mph in a 70 mph zone," he said.

Yet as *Delano* progresses, Dunne warms up toward Chavez. Dunne understands the hopes deposited in Chavez and the power of his spirituality based on Christian values, his messianic drive, and his shrewd yet polarizing strategies as a leader. But he sees Chavez less as a solution than as a mystery. "The curious thing about Cesar Chavez," Dunne states, "is that he is as little understood by those who would canonize him as by those who would condemn him." Dunne perceives him, with some ambivalence, as a rural folk hero.

> To the saint-makers, Chavez seemed the perfect candidate. His crusade was devoid of the ambiguities of urban conflict. With the farm workers there were no nagging worries about the mugging down the block, the rape across the street, the car boosted in front of the house. It was a cause populated by simple Mexican peasants with noble agrarian ideas, not by surly unemployables with low IQs and Molotov cocktails. . . . The saintly virtues [Chavez] had aplenty; it is doubtful that the media would have been attracted to him were it not for those virtues, and without the attention of the media the strike could not have survived. But Chavez also had the virtues of the labor leader, less applauded publicly perhaps, but no less admirable in the rough going—a will of iron, a certain deviousness, an ability to hang tough in the clinches.

What is most striking to me about the picture that emerges of Chavez in the last sections of *Delano* is that it is in the past tense. Dunne sees the *huelga* in Delano as a fait accompli. He predicts that in urban centers what he calls "an ethnic and cultural pride ungerminated for generations" will explode one day.

Drive down Whittier Boulevard in East Los Angeles, a slum in the Southern California manner, street after street of tiny bungalows and parched lawns and old cars, a grid of monotony. The signs are unnoticed at first, catching the eye only after the second or third sighting, whitewashed on fences and abandoned storefronts, the paint splattered and uneven, signs painted on the run in the dark of the night, *"Es mejor morir de pie que vivir de rodillas"*—"Better to die standing than live on your knees." The words are those of Emiliano Zapata, but the spirit that wrote them was fired by Cesar Chavez.

Dunne analyzes the picture before him and connects the dots. He talks about issues of ethnicity and about the low self-esteem he sees in the Mexican-American population. And he understands the allure of extremism. "What the barrio is learning from the blacks is the political sex appeal of violence," he affirms. ". . . The vocabulary of the dispossessed is threat and riot, the Esperanto of a crisis-reacting society, italicizing the poverty and discrimination and social deprivation in a way that no funded study or government commission ever could." Dunne doesn't emphasize how charged the word *Chicano* is, but he is certainly aware that the concept of assimilation as previous waves of newcomers understood it has changed dramatically. Possibly because racism and discrimination are rampant, or because Mexico is just *del otro lado,* on the other side, the pressure to conform to the mainstream cultural patterns in the United States is no longer there. But Dunne's prognosis is local. He mentions the term *la causa* but doesn't expand it beyond the Southwest. There is little connection in *Delano* between the NFWA and the Puerto Rican Young Lords. This limitation, needless to say, isn't Dunne's exclusively. The entire civil rights era continues to be viewed today in black and white. Few (Dunne among them) were able to prophesy that Chavez's movement would inaugurate "brownness" as a mode of thinking.

Dunne's account was published in book form by Farrar, Straus and Giroux in 1967, with black-and-white photographs by Ted Streshinsky that are considerably more biased toward the NFWA than the reportage. Four years later, a revised, updated edition appeared in which Dunne brought his chronicle full circle by explaining how the strike had been resolved and how Chavez had moved from grapes to lettuces. By the mid-1970s that edition was out of print, and the Delano strike was virtually forgotten. But since the mid-1980s, a young generation of Latinos, a vast number of them of Mexican descent (in the year 2005 approximately sixteen out of every twenty Latinos had roots in Mexico), has come to the fore, seeking clues to understand its recent and remote past in the United States. On the surface they look to be less connected with radicalism than with the embrace of middle-class commodities. The barrio might even now be a time bomb, but pop culture—reggaetón, Hollywood, sports—allows the disenfranchised to feel attached to the nation's soul. And war: the number of *mexicanos* in the armed forces is considerable. Even if *la huelga* isn't a daily topic of conversation for them, their need to identify heroes and benchmarks is legitimate. The conditions of itinerant farm workers in the Southwest have changed somewhat in the interim, not always for the better. Growers have embraced mechanization to increase production. The workers' living provisions are, for the most part, less miserable. The wages have increased, though they've never kept up with inflation. The work still requires long hours of backbreaking physical effort, and pesticides still undermine workers' health. Worse, the perception of Mexicans in the United States as subhuman is more pervasive than ever, as attested by the labyrinthine and never-ending national debate on immigration. *Parasites* is the noun used by a prominent CNN commentator.

After Dunne concludes his reportage and gets back on Highway 99, he reflects on the effect of Chavez on the people. In the end, he realizes, the strike didn't (as he had predicted) get mired in quicksand. He wonders at the impact of the newly founded Chicano labor management and its connection to cultural assimilation. "Denied to blacks," he states, "assimilation for years robbed the Chicano community of a nucleus of leadership. Today the forfeiture of this newly acquired cultural awareness seems to the young Chicano a prohibitive price to pay." But these gains would be difficult to sustain. While the 1970s would be a decade of political consolidation, the 1980s and 1990s would deplete the ideological capital accumulated by Chavez and his peers. As Dunne leaves Delano, he does see that bumper stickers that read "Boycott California Grapes" and "Buy California Grapes" are now fading.

Ilan Stavans
McAllen, Texas,
August 2007

DELANO

ONE

Highway 99 drops out of the dun-colored foothills of the Tehachapis north of Los Angeles and for the next five hundred miles cuts straight as a plumb line up through the Great Central Valley of California. It is a landscape remarkable only in its flatness, its absolute absence of distinguishable topography. Except for the few cold, gray months of winter, a deadening heat lies over the dull green fields that stretch from the Sierrra Nevada on the east to the Coast Range on the west. An occasional glimpse of an irrigation canal takes on, for the driver passing through the Valley, the aspect of scenery. Breaking the monotony are a succession of towns, but for all intents and purposes they might be the same, some larger, some smaller, yet all seemingly grafted onto the land by the same hand. Beyond those, all that saves the driver from highway narcosis are the big rotating sprinklers and the yellow crop dusters floating lazily in the bleached blue sky until they sweep over the fields trailing clouds of Ortho-K and all the other insecticides that anyone who watches billboards on Highway 99 could name in his sleep.

In its heat and in its flatness, it all suggests a vacuum of the human will, but the feeling, like the Valley itself, deceives, for this is the heartland of the richest industry in California, a $4.08 billion-a-year industry that goes by the name "agribusiness." From this state and largely from this

Valley comes forty-three percent of the fruit and vegetables sold in the United States, more cotton than is grown in Georgia, tomatoes, peanuts, asparagus, apples, plums, grapes, sugar beets. In Kern, Tulare, and Fresno counties alone, the annual crop is worth in excess of one billion dollars. It is growing which gives the Valley year its rhythm. It is growing which gives Valley life its particular tone, growing which has enabled Valley people to remain largely insulated from what industrial America thinks and does and worries about. The concerns of people in Tulare and Madera and Merced are a way of life removed from those of people in the space industries of Southern California or on the assembly line at River Rouge or tending the Bessemer converters along the Monongahela. The prevailing ethic is that of the nineteenth-century frontier. And it is precisely this rhythm, this tone, this insulation, this ethic which made the Valley unable to understand an intense, unschooled Mexican-American named Cesar Chavez and the bitter labor strike which broke out in the grape vineyards surrounding the little Valley town of Delano in the fall of 1965.

It is in no way extraordinary that the Valley was unable to understand Cesar Chavez. He belongs to that inarticulate subculture of farm workers upon whom the Valley depends but whose existence does not impinge heavily on the Valley consciousness. Their world is one of side roads and labor camps, of anonymous toil under a blistering sun. The very existence of farm workers is a conundrum. Because they have never been effectively organized, they have never been included under legislation that safeguards the rights of industrial workers; because they are excluded from the machinery of collective bargaining, they have never been able to organize effectively. Nearly half the male workers are Mexican, and during the harvest, when wives and children spill into the fields to pick the crop before it rots, the percentage of Mexican-Americans swells to over seventy percent. Once the crop is in, they are as welcome as a drought, regarded in each community as no more than a threat to the relief rolls. Migrating with the harvest from crop to crop, they work an average of only 134 days a year. Eighty-four percent earn less than the federal poverty level of $3,100; the average annual income is $1,378. So pervasive is their poverty that in Fresno County, over eighty percent of the welfare cases come from farm labor families.

This was the birthright of Cesar Chavez. He went on the road at the age of ten, eking out a seventh-grade education in some three dozen farm community schools. "That winter of 1938 I had to walk to school barefoot through the mud, we were so poor," he has recalled. "After school, we fished in the canal and cut wild mustard greens—otherwise we would have starved. Everyone else left the camp we were living in, but we had no money for transportation. When everyone else left, they shut off the lights, so we sat around in the dark. We finally got a few dollars from some relatives in Arizona and bought enough gas for our old Studebaker to get us to Los Angeles. Our car broke down in L.A. and my mother sold crocheting in the street to raise the money for enough gas to get to Brawley. We lived three days in our car in Brawley before we found a house we could afford to rent. Next winter, we were stranded in Oxnard and had to spend the winter in a tent.

We went to bed at dusk because there was no light. My mother and father got up at 5:30 in the morning to go pick peas. It cost seventy cents to go to the fields and back and some days they did not even make enough money for their transportation. To help out, my brother and I started looking along the highway for empty cigarette packages, for the tinfoil. Every day we would look for cigarette packages and we made a huge ball of tinfoil that weighed eighteen pounds. Then we sold it to a Mexican junk dealer for enough money to buy a pair of tennis shoes and two sweatshirts."

The words might have come from *The Grapes of Wrath*, and, indeed, to read and hear about Delano and Cesar Chavez in the months after September 1965 was to have a curious sense of *déjà vu*. The Delano strike appeared to have no kinship with the institutionalized formalities of most contemporary labor disputes. There was no ritual of collective bargaining, no negotiating table around which it was difficult to tell the managers of money from the hewers of wood and the carriers of water, no talk of guidelines and fringe benefits and the national weal, no professional mediators, on leave from academe at a hundred dollars a day and all expenses paid, plugged in by special telephone lines to the Oval Room at the White House. The strike in Delano seemed primed by earlier, more violent memories. It might have been a direct descendent of the Pullman Strike of 1894, when thirty workers were gunned down by state militiamen in the rail yards of Chicago, of the sit-ins staged by the fledgling United Auto Workers in 1937, when Walter Reuther was beaten and kicked on the picket line and then thrown down a flight of stairs outside the Ford Motor Company's River Rouge plant. Even the cause of Cesar Chavez and his strikers seemed particularly superannuated in contemporary America—the demand of workers for the right to organize.

But since that fall of 1965, Chavez's demand has riven the town of Delano. There, for the first time in thirty years, union activity was met with the cry of "Communism" and a town was mobilized to combat the Red Menace of labor organizers. There, embattled growers, untouched by labor's consolidation over the past three decades, were acting as if the Wobblies were still the nation's number-one threat. There the AFL-CIO was mouthing the jargon of "capitalist exploitation"; there the strident voice of the radical Left was heard; there the beards and sandals and dirty fingernails provoked the shrill charge of "outside agitators." There clergymen invoked Scripture to denounce each other as "Godless," growers clutched the American flag and sang "The Star-Spangled Banner," strikers waved red banners and chanted "We Shall Overcome." There each side declared itself innocent of violence, yet anonymous telephone callers breathed threats, fires lit the night, and shotgun blasts split the midnight silence.

The song was an old one, the lyric curiously irrelevant. In that sun-seared Valley town, the mythology of the thirties had been superimposed on a situation of the sixties. And yet, for the first time, the myths were threatening to unravel the social fabric of agrarian California. As it happens, I married into the Valley, into a family that began farming there in the days of the Gold Rush, and so in the summer of 1966 I went to Delano to see a town beleaguered by forces it did not understand, to see how and why Cesar Chavez had become the right man at the right place at what was, sadly, both the right and the wrong time.

TWO

"HUNGRY? TIRED? CAR TROUBLE? NEED GAS?" the road sign
beckons from the shoulder of Highway 99. "STOP IN DE-
LANO." Until the strike began in September, 1965, there
were few other reasons to stop in Delano.

Geographically, Delano (pronounced Delayno) is located
in the San Joaquin Valley, that part of the Great Central
Valley drained by the San Joaquin River. It was founded
by the Southern Pacific Railroad in 1873 and the SP, its
eye characteristically trained on favors from Washington,
named its new rail site after Christopher Delano, Secretary of the Interior under Ulysses S. Grant. For nearly fifty
years the town languished in the semidesert of northern
Kern County, just south of the Tulare County line. It was
not until after the turn of the century, when land was becoming scarce in California, that farmers saw the possibilities in tapping the reservoirs of underground water beneath Delano. With irrigation, Delano began to flourish.
The climate was perfect for grapes, and with the added
water from the state and federally sponsored Central Valley Project, the town was gradually enclosed in a 37,000
acre vise of Ribiers, Parlettes, Muscats, Almerias, Emperors, and Thompsons.

It is not the grapes, however, but the grape growers that
make Delano unique in the Valley. In the 1920's, the climate and fertility of the local vineyards attracted to Del-

ano a contingent of Yugoslavian emigrants who had tended
grapes for generations along the Adriatic. Today these
Yugoslavians, mostly second generation with a smattering
of first-generation patriarchs, set the social tone of Delano.
The signs on the packing sheds and along the county roads
tell the story—Gutunich, Radovich, Pandol, Caratan; in
the Delano telephone book, there are twenty-three "Zaninovich" listings alone. The Yugoslavians have intermarried
and crossbred and made a world unto themselves. This is
not that part of the Valley where the growers belong to the
country club and their daughters to the Junior League.
There is no country club at all in Delano; the social life of
the growers revolves around the Elks Club and the Slav
Hall.

Today the population of Delano is approximately 14,-
000 and it is split almost evenly between the "Anglos,"
who live east of the freeway, and the Mexicans, the Filipinos, and the few Negroes who live west of Highway 99.
(The term "Anglo," as it is used in the Valley, encompasses
all whites, save Mexicans, whether they be Christian or
Jew, of eastern or southern European origin.) The town
has twenty-eight churches, four elementary schools, one
high school, a general hospital with forty beds, a twice-
weekly newspaper, four banks, eight doctors, four den-
tists, three optometrists, and two chiropractors. The East
Side is somnolent and well-kept and no different from any
one of a dozen other Valley towns. Most of Delano's busi-
nesses are located here, the kind whose owners attend the
Lions Club or Rotary International luncheons once a week
in the Blue Room at the Stardust Motel. There is an International Harvester franchise, a Bank of America branch,
two movie theaters (one of which shows Mexican films

twice a week), several motels, a Fosters' Freeze, Marshall's Pharmacy, Mulligan's Furniture Store, but no bookstore; the nearest is in Bakersfield, thirty miles to the south. Little distinguishes one East Side residential street from another; block succeeds block of pastel ranch-style bungalows, their exteriors already faded and pockmarked from falling plaster. And then there is The Terrace, the crescent-shaped silk-stocking district of Delano, where the houses are a little bigger, the lots a little larger, and the sunflowers a little taller. Some of the children of the big growers live on The Terrace, as does the president of the local bank, in a mock colonial house which is the only conventional two-story dwelling in view.

At first impression, the West Side looks little different from the East Side. But slowly it becomes apparent that Highway 99 is a social as well as a geographical line of demarcation between the two Delanos. It is not just that the skins of the people on the West Side are darker. The bungalows are shabbier and the cars are older. Occasionally a drainage ditch is exposed, and there are more potholes in the streets. Just west of the Southern Pacific tracks is a strip of lo-ball and draw-poker parlors with names like Divina's Four Deuces, the Monte Carlo, the Guadalajara. Every night, old Mexicans in stained straw field hats and faded work shirts sit stolidly around the tables watching the cards passed to them. It was in this area that Delano's once flourishing red-light district was located. One night in the Four Deuces I asked an old field worker what he thought of the situation in Delano, and he answered, "This used to be a good town before." It turned out that he meant before the construction of the freeway leveled the red-light district; the strike, in his opinion, was only a further and somewhat anticlimactic step in the decline of Delano.

The headquarters of Cesar Chavez's National Farm Workers' Association at 102 Albany Street is no more nor less seedy than the rest of the West Side. The building itself has had a checkered history. Before the NFWA moved in, it had been at various times a grocery and a Jehovah's Witnesses Hall. At almost any hour of the day or night, the NFWA's rolling stock—decrepit automobiles which seem glued together with spit and baling wire from the discards of some manic used-car lot—are parked outside. The cars are easily identifiable in Delano and are at times handy targets. A few days before my arrival in town, a Rambler driven by Chavez's administrative assistant, the Reverend James Drake of the California Migrant Ministry, which has been intimately involved with the strike since its outset, was shot up by assailants unknown, who peppered its chassis and blew out its windows with shotgun pellets while it stood empty outside 102 Albany.

The interior of NFWA headquarters is a dusty, chaotic shambles of plywood partitions, mimeograph machines, and battered desks. Pasted in the window are paper reproductions of the NFWA's splendidly barbaric coat of arms —a black eagle on a scarlet field on which is printed the Spanish word for strike, HUELGA. The coat of arms is strongly reminiscent of the symbol for the New Deal's National Recovery Administration, but among the townspeople of Delano it is invariably spoken of as "Chavez's Trotsky flag." On every available inch of wall, there is a profusion of maps, telephone numbers, picket instructions, and cartoons which unfailingly depict the growers in planter's hats and sunglasses, smoking fat cigars and carrying bullwhips. Strewn around the outer office are copies of the *Butterick Home Catalogue* and back issues of *Coed* magazine. (One day I came upon a hefty Mexican woman, with most of her teeth missing, engrossed in a *Coed* article entitled "How to Act on a Double Date" and containing such instructions as: "Bring your coat to the table. Tipping is expensive.") The only thing in repose in the whole office is a statue of the Virgin of Guadalupe, patron saint of the NFWA and of the strike.

Tacked to the back wall is a single sheet of paper which, though a joke, attests more than anything else in the room to what life has been like in Delano for the past year. On it are listed the recipients of "The Order of the Purple Grape —the official decoration of the NFWA for injury in action." Among the recipients were a volunteer who had had a shotgun fired over his head by a security guard at one of the ranches, a striker narrowly missed by another shotgun blast, and a one-armed NFWA supporter who had been beaten up by a grower. Perhaps the most illuminating example was that of the Reverend David Havens of the Migrant Ministry. A month or so after the strike started, when the growers had begun bringing in workers from other parts of California and out of state to replace those who had walked out, Havens went out on the picket line one day and, in defiance of deputies from the Kern County sheriff's office, began reading Jack London's famous "Definition of a Strikebreaker":

After God had finished the rattlesnake, the toad and the vampire, He had some awful substance left with which he made a strikebreaker. A strikebreaker is a two-legged animal with a corkscrew soul, a waterlogged brain and a combination backbone made of jelly and glue. When a strikebreaker comes down the street, men turn their backs and angels weep in Heaven and the devil shuts the gates of Hell to keep him out. Judas Iscariot was a gentleman compared to the strikebreaker. The modern strikebreaker sells his birthright, his country, his wife, his children and his fellow men for an unfulfilled promise from his employer, trust or corporation. There is nothing lower than a strikebreaker.

No sooner had Havens finished than he was arrested by the sheriff's deputies for disturbing the peace. The case was later dismissed in court.

I knew little about the care and cultivation of grapes when I arrived in Delano in the summer of 1966, save for the fact that table grapes presented a greater opportunity for union organizers than any other seasonal crops. Unlike lettuce or asparagus, grapes require attention for some ten months a year. They must be sprayed, trimmed, and girdled. Each process takes a certain degree of skill. As a result, the labor force is relatively stable. There are few migrants, except during the harvest, and since the residents can put in nearly a full year's work, their income levels are accordingly higher. As the richest of the poor, they are less apathetic than migrants whose overriding considerations are the next job, the next meal, and hence more susceptible to an organizing effort.

A day or so after I checked into the Stardust Motel, I drove down to the DiGiorgio Corporation's ranch in Arvin, some thirty miles south of Delano, to see how grapes are grown and how a huge corporation ranch is run. The Arvin ranch has 9,000 acres, slightly less than half planted in grapes, the rest in plums, potatoes, asparagus, cotton, peanuts, wheat, barley, and black-eyed beans. Unlike DiGiorgio's 4,400-acre Sierra Vista ranch in Delano, it was not then being struck. I was met by Joseph A. DiGiorgio, a vice president of the DiGiorgio Corporation and head of its farming operation. (Farming accounts for less than ten percent of DiGiorgio's annual sales of $230 million; the bulk of its income derives from food processing and grocery wholesaling.) Joseph DiGiorgio is a short, tanned, muscular man in late middle age, with the classic profile of a Renaissance pope. He wore a straw planter's hat with a madras band, a neatly pressed blue buttoned-down sport shirt and work shoes so brightly polished that they would have done credit to a member of a military drill team. He suggested that the best way to see the ranch operate was to drive around with him for the rest of the day, and so I got into his car. There was a two-way radio in the car, and periodically through the morning and afternoon he would call back instructions to his office and receive reports from field foremen.

DiGiorgio explained that the grape season is progressive, proceeding from Coachella and Borrego over to the high desert in Arizona, then back to Arvin, up to Delano, and on up the Valley. In the best of years, the seasons do not overlap and there is no price break, but when they do, as they did in 1965, so many grapes hit the market at the same time that the price plummets. Thus, though 1965 was a vintage year in quality and quantity, many grape ranchers took a serious beating. We passed through vineyards of Cardinals, Thompsons, Ribiers, Red Malagas, Emperors, Almerias, Calmerias, and Muscats, and at each we stopped to sample the grapes. Some were quite tart and not yet ready for picking. I was told that it takes five years to bring a vine into full production and that the productive life of a quality vine ranges from twenty-five to thirty years. Then the vines are pulled out and the land reworked for several years with other crops, such as cotton or potatoes. Throughout the year, there is constant cultural work to be done. Girdling is one example. A strip, or girdle, of bark is cut out of the vine, disrupting its natural water intake and outflow and thus forcing the moisture already in the vine up into the berries, swelling their size. Girdling is done strictly on a piecework basis, the workers making two or three cents a vine.

We drove down a dirt lane and stopped by a picking stand. There was a sunshade over the stand, and a radio playing Mexican music. DiGiorgio showed me the tally sheet for one crew of field workers. The day before, the crew had picked 117 lugs of grapes, an average of 2.17 boxes an hour, giving the workers an hourly wage of $1.73. "It's hard work," he said. It was an understatement. The workers hunch under the vines like ducks. There is no air, making the intense heat all but unbearable. Gnats and bugs swarm out from under the leaves. Some workers wear face masks; others, handkerchiefs knotted around their heads to catch the sweat. I asked if there were not some way to automate the picking process. He shook his head and brought me under a vine to explain why. "If it were just a matter of picking, it might be feasible," he said. "You could do it for raisins or for wine grapes, but there are too many quality checks for table grapes." He clipped a bunch of grapes and handed it to me. "A picker has got to check color, the size of the berry, the size of the bunch, and trim bad berries before a bunch can be packed," he went on. "How are you going to mechanize these functions?" He examined the bunch and threw it away. "That one would never pass muster."

On the way back to lunch, we passed a plum orchard where a bulldozer was neatly uprooting trees and laying them in symmetrical rows. The trees had been planted in 1947, I was told, but they were no longer economically productive because of poor root stock. I asked if I could see one of the labor camps before lunch. Arvin employs Mexicans, Filipinos, Puerto Ricans, Negroes, and Anglos, and, as they are at every large ranch, the workers are segregated by nationality. At the height of the harvest, the work force runs to a peak of between 1,200 and 1,400 men, dropping to between 400 and 500 during slack periods. "Our basic concept here is to have enough crop diversification so that we'll be harvesting ten months a year," Di-Giorgio said. "That gives greater employment."

He chose to show me a Mexican camp. The mess hall reminded me of the army. In the kitchen, cooks were preparing a lunch of steak, corn, and tortillas. (A machine stamps out over three thousand tortillas a day in the Mexican camp.) "This is just a normal meal," he said. "Nothing special." Outside, I saw a cluster of older living quarters with pipe chimneys, but I was steered into a newer building which still smelled of wet paint. The building was air-conditioned and accommodated forty-eight men. In the bathroom there were four toilets, six showers, and eight sinks. Four men live in a room. They sleep on cots and have their own wardrobes and shelves. Room and board costs $2.25 a day, which is deducted from their pay. There was nothing shabby about the building, but it was as cold and as impersonal as a barracks. I asked one of the workers how he liked living there. "It's like any place else," he said. "Some of the people are real clean and some are hogs."

We ate lunch in the supervisors' dining room, which was separated by a plywood wall from the Anglo mess hall. Lunch was cold cuts, a hot vegetable, Jello, and iced tea. We sat at a large table with six or eight ranch department heads who talked shop all through the meal—titration tests, irrigating plans, and crop yields. Someone made a joke about sour grapes and there was a good deal of mechanical laughter. Many of the ranch supervisors, DiGiorgio told me later, were the sons of Dust Bowl Okies who had begun working for the company as pickers. They averaged eighteen years with DiGiorgio. "It's hard to get good young people from Davis and the other agricultural colleges these days," he said. "They all want too much money and think they should start off with my job. They know all the answers, so maybe they're better off working as county agents."

After lunch, DiGiorgio showed me Arvin's family housing, which, depending on the size of the unit, rents for five dollars, seven-fifty, or ten dollars a month. There was a playground with a baseball field and a tennis court. "We fix up the tennis court every couple of years," he said, "but they never use it except to play basketball on." We then drove to the packing house. It is an enormous building, roughly the size of two football fields. Trailer trucks were backed up along the side of the shed. On the second floor, there were rooms where the truckers could sleep while their trailers were being loaded. We watched the packing from a balcony outside the shed office. The packers were women and most were the wives and daughters of field help. They packed each box of plums and grapes by size and quality of the fruit, picking it off a conveyor belt, examining it, and then placing it in the appropriate box. It seemed a tedious, exacting job. Bunches of grapes that did not meet the quality standards for table grapes were culled and sent down another conveyor, which transported them outside, where they were dumped into gondolas for transport to the winery. Once boxed, the good fruit was placed in huge pre-cooling storage areas where the field heat could fade, giving the fruit longer transit and shelf life.

Before I left Arvin, Joseph DiGiorgio drove me out to see what the land looked like when his uncle, the founder of the company, bought it nearly fifty years ago. We were at the edge of the ranch property line. There was nothing but sand, sagebrush, and cactus. With some pride, DiGiorgio told me he had helped level the land himself. As we drove back to my car, we passed an arbor of blackberry bushes. It was a biological control project. Parasites lived in the bushes during the winter and then spread out from the arbor in the summer, laying their eggs on the eggs of harmful insects, thus acting as a natural pesticide. I remarked that farming was certainly complicated, that it took a combination scientist, engineer, and agronomist to keep a ranch running.

"Nobody stops to think of the farmer's problems," DiGiorgio said. "We have a tremendous capital investment in packing and boxmaking and storing and mechanical equipment, in trucks and cooling systems. Rain can spoil an entire crop, and when a crop overlaps, as it did last year in grapes, the price breaks because of overproduction. Our profit margin is at the mercy of the elements. We've got to know when to plant, what to plant, when to irrigate, when to rotate, when to pick. Five years from now, is the public going to go for a certain type grape we plant today?" The question was rhetorical, and as we shook hands he answered himself. "It's a gamble, that's all it is."

THREE

So indeed was the strike. By the time I got to Delano, ten months after the first walkout, it had gone into a holding phase, somewhat akin to the trench warfare of World War I. Except for occasional forays into violence, both sides held fast, hurling little more than a constant stream of epithets at each other. The mood of the town was sullen and suspicious, especially toward outsiders. One day after I had been there for nearly two weeks, I was stopped on the street by a leader of Citizens for Facts from Delano, a local group formed to counteract what they considered prejudiced, inaccurate, and pro-Chavez strike publicity. "I hear you're going to write a slanted story," he said. When I asked how he had come to this conclusion, he replied, "Well, you've been seeing Chavez, haven't you?" He gave me a look of impassive disbelief when I told him that some of the people at NFWA headquarters thought I was committing treason by even venturing over to the East Side.

In both camps there was a morbid fascination with what the other side was thinking and doing, and at times I felt almost like a Red Cross emissary passing between the lines under a flag of truce with parcels of quite meaningless information. Gradually, I grew inured to and versed in the demonology of Delano. There was, to begin with, a local *lingua franca*. Any reference to the strike on the part of the growers was prefaced by the phrase "so-called." A request for reportorial objectivity meant don't-cross-the-freeway. There were also various articles of faith. Not only his supporters but Chavez himself swore the organized opposition on the East Side was led by ex-prostitutes. This was matched by the town's conviction that the various Protestant ministers who had come to town to aid Chavez had "turned their collars around" to masquerade as Catholic priests among the predominantly Catholic Mexicans.

It had taken ten months of attrition for Delano to arrive at this state of paranoia. At the beginning of the strike, Delano, with some forbearance, had looked at Chavez merely as an upstart. His first grievance was economic and the town conceded he had a case. At that time, the average wage in the Valley was $1.20 an hour, plus a piece-rate of ten cents a lug of grapes picked. Chavez demanded $1.40 and twenty-five cents a basket, plus enforcement of the standard working conditions prescribed by state law. These laws were mainly concerned with adequate field sanitation facilities and were in many cases quite casually broken. At one Valley ranch, according to a woman worker, the field boss charged his hands twenty-five cents for a cup of water, and at a farm in the Delano area, sixty-seven workers were forced to drink from one cup, which was an empty beer can. Nor did this second ranch have the portable field toilets required by state law. Here the women workers were forced to squat down several rows over from where they were picking. They also maintained that their foreman used to sneak after them and watch them.

These were grievances that some quarters in Delano were willing to consider legitimate—until Chavez also demanded that the growers recognize the NFWA as bargaining agent for all the field workers in the area. The growers flatly refused. Only a handful of the thirty-eight growers in the Delano area even bothered to open the registered letters Chavez sent out on the eve of the strike asking for negotiations. When later I asked one of them why he had not acknowledged Chavez's letter, he answered, "Why, hell, I didn't get that letter until 12:30 and that meeting was supposed to be at eleven o'clock in the morning. Now you tell me, how can I get to a meeting that began an hour and a half before?" Certain that they held all the cards, the growers pretended that neither Chavez nor the strike existed.

At any other time, this tactic might have prevailed. But the civil-rights movement in other parts of the country had pricked the national conscience. Whatever one felt about the movement itself, few would deny that a vast body of the American public were second-class citizens, none more so than the Mexican-American farm workers. The movement had evolved a methodology of protest perfectly suited to conditions in Delano, as well as a cadre of workers willing to come there to put their special skills to work. They were mostly white college students for whom Delano was the only game in town; the civil-rights movement in the South had been taken over by Negroes grown increasingly sensitive to the fact of white domination, and the anti-Vietnam struggle was an abstraction with relatively few opportunities for confrontation.

Recognizing the need for outside support, Chavez, late in September of 1965, went to Stanford and Berkeley to drum up backing from student activists and invited workers from the Congress of Racial Equality and the Student Nonviolent Coordinating Committee to come to Delano to help organize the picket lines. Most of the picket captains in the early days of the strike were SNCC and CORE volunteers. "You just couldn't have someone who had never been on a picket line before," one of the NFWA leaders told me. "We needed somebody who could talk to the cops —or who had the confidence to talk to the cops. The Mexicans couldn't handle it at first. They had to be trained into the job." The logistics of picketing over thirty ranches were staggering. "It's like striking an industrial plant that has a thousand entrance gates and is four hundred square miles large," one SNCC worker said. "And if that isn't bad enough, you don't know each morning where the plant will be, or where the gates are, or whether it will be open or closed, or what wages will be offered that day."

With two-way radios lent by SNCC and CORE, scout cars would spread out around Delano before dawn, looking for evidence that certain vineyards would be worked that day. The signs were packing boxes stacked by the side of the road or a foreman's pickup parked down a lane. Information also came from inside the camps and from a few friendly truck drivers who told the NFWA where they were taking the crews. "Scouting you never did by yourself," I was told by Wendy Goepel, a limpid, childlike young woman who was one of the first volunteers to arrive in Delano. "I was driven off the road one day, someone just forced me off. After that, I never went out by myself." When a field looked promising, word was radioed back to NFWA headquarters and a caravan of roving pickets would be dispatched to the appointed rendezvous. Often the growers, in the early weeks of the strike, would see them coming and take their workers out of that particular field. One grower cruised over Delano in his private plane on the lookout for the picket caravan, and when he spotted it from the air he would radio its location to his crew on the ground. Some growers would move their workers from the roadside to the middle of a vineyard so that they would not see the pickets. Others drove down the edge of their property line with spraying machines, shooting insecticide and fertilizer on the pickets, or gunned over the roadside in tractors, raising dust to choke the strikers. Growers played car radios at top volume to drown out the pickets' shouts of *"Huelga"* or else placed a line of automobiles between the picket line and their workers so that the strikers could not see the field help.

The pickets were bound by an oath of nonviolence, and at times it was sorely tried. Growers walked up and down the picket line, stamping on the toes of the strikers, tripping them up, or elbowing them in the ribs. Augustin Lira, one of the pickets, told me that a grower seemed to have singled him out as his own special project. "He'd come up to me and say, nice like, 'What are you doing here, boy?' and then he'd kick me." On the first day of the strike, a grower's son-in-law wrenched a sign from one picket, stood it against a fence, and calmly blew it apart with his rifle. One day James Drake of the Migrant Ministry was walking in town when a grower stopped his car in front of him, got out, and began pummeling him in the middle of the street. I asked Drake what he had done to protect himself and he answered, "Nothing, he was just a little guy."

Despite the NFWA's oath, however, the violence was not all that one-sided. "The strike is a farce," one nonstriking woman worker said. "It's a phony and a hoax. Those of us who have resisted the union organizing efforts have been beaten, shot at, deliberately run down by cars driven by so-called strikers. Twelve hoodlums forced my husband to go to the union hall, where he was told we had better cooperate or else. The union knew we had been to the authorities. With no other means of protecting ourselves, we were forced to obtain a restraining order. This cost us our savings." One NFWA supporter aimed his car at three growers standing in the road, scattering them like tenpins, with the result that one grower had his leg broken. Piles of packing boxes were mysteriously put to the torch in the night and the Kern County sheriff's office discovered that Chavez supporters had purchased 4,000 marbles, which they were firing with slingshots at strikebreakers in the field. Rocks were thrown through windows in strikebreakers' houses, and picket signs set up on lawns reading "A SCAB LIVES HERE." One nine-year-old girl was told that unless her father came out of the fields her house would be burned down.

The attitude of the Kern and Tulare county law-enforcement agencies during those early days of the strike was, in the words of one observer, "scrupulously ambivalent." Growers had little difficulty obtaining restraining orders against picketing from friendly local authorities, even though these orders were usually vacated at the next level of appeal. Shortly after the Reverend Havens was arrested for reading Jack London's "Definition of A Strikebreaker," an injunction was issued against the shouting of the word "*Huelga*" on the picket line. Almost immediately, Chavez supporters informed the Kern County sheriff's office that they were going to make a test case of the ruling.

The following morning, the protesters held a meeting at NFWA headquarters to map out details. One of the NFWA staff informed the sheriff's office where the demonstration was to be held, so that deputies would be on hand to make the test arrests. Then the caravan started out. There were no workers at the first stop, and scout cars fanned out over the nearby roads until one reported a crew working at a ranch owned by W. B. Camp. The procession to the Camp ranch had a carnival atmosphere. The workers were followed by reporters, sheriff's cars, and a paddy wagon. At the ranch, a picket line was set up and the demonstrators began to chant, "*Huelga, huelga, huelga.*" For nearly a half hour, the deputies took pictures of the pickets. Finally Sergeant Gerald Dodd took over a loudspeaker and told the pickets that they were engaged in unlawful assembly and ordered them to disperse. He issued the same warning personally to each demonstrator and then had it read in Spanish. At last, the arrests began. Almost jokingly, the pickets allowed themselves to be packed into the paddy wagon. They did not lie down or go limp. There was standing room only in the van, and several demonstrators were put in squad cars for the trip to the county jail. Only fifteen of the forty-four pickets arrested were from the Delano area, bolstering Delano's charges of "outside agitators." But the NFWA won its point. The case was dismissed and pickets were allowed to go on shouting "*Huelga.*"

One day Chavez and a Catholic priest from Sacramento flew over the vineyards trying to make contact, via a bullhorn, with workers out of range of roadside pickets; they were both arrested for violating the grower's air space. In some cases, the police seemed to go out of their way to harass the roving pickets. "I'd drive a different way every day, but the cops would always stop me," Augustin Lira told me. "They'd tell me my lights weren't working or my signals were out of order or that I didn't make a signal when I turned. The cops always had tape recorders and cameras. I'd tell the people in the fields, 'These tape recorders, these cameras, they don't scare me, they shouldn't scare you.' "

Cameras, in fact, seemed to be indispensable artifacts of keeping the peace in Delano. Police photographed everyone who walked on a picket line, and took down the license number of every car parked in front of NFWA headquarters. The numbers were checked out with the California Department of Motor Vehicles in Sacramento, and the names were then sent to state and federal authorities to see if the owner had a record. With this information, the Kern County sheriff's office was able to make up a card file of 5,000 suspected strike supporters. Each card showed the supporter's name, criminal record if there was one, association with civil-rights groups if known, and a mug shot from the dossier of picket pictures if name and photo could be matched up. In one case, pickets were threatened by workers still in the fields and, instead of arresting the workers who made the threats, the Kern County sheriff's office arrested the pickets. It was this legal concept which precipitated the following exchange between United States Senator Robert Kennedy and Kern County Sheriff Roy Galyen when the United States Senate Subcommittee on Migratory Labor, in March, 1966, held hearings in Delano on the strike situation:

KENNEDY:
"What did you charge them with?"
GALYEN:
"Violation of—unlawful assembly."

KENNEDY:

"I think that's most interesting. Who told you that they were going to riot?"

GALYEN:

"The men right out in the field that they were talking to said, 'If you don't get them out of here, we're going to cut their hearts out.' So rather than let them get cut, we removed the cause."

KENNEDY:

"This is the most interesting concept, I think. How can you arrest somebody if they haven't violated the law?"

GALYEN:

"They're ready to violate the law."

KENNEDY:

"Can I suggest that the sheriff read the Constitution of the United States?"

FOUR

How Delano reached this impasse is a primer in California agriculture, present and past. To this day, the administrative obstacles in organizing farm labor are formidable. The workers are generally hired by labor contractors, who recruit them off the street and lease them to individual growers. (This practice is less prevalent in grapes than in other crops, because of the relative stability of the grape labor force.) Migrants are usually housed in labor camps on the grower's property; organizers can gain access only by trespassing or by obtaining the permission of the grower, who is unlikely to give it. Under these conditions, a strike is virtually impossible. "A strike presupposes the existence of some sort of framework, some sort of ground rules for negotiation," says Henry Anderson, chairman of Citizens for Farm Labor. "It presupposes the existence of collective-bargaining machinery. There is no such machinery in agriculture. Not more than one in a hundred California farm workers is represented by anyone in any meaningful sense. There is no way to find out by whom the farm workers would like to be represented, if anyone. No one has a list of workers who are attached to the grape industry; where they live; or anything that needs to be known about them if there is to be any sort of contract covering them. These are some of the consequences of the fact that agriculture is excluded from the Labor-Management Relations Act of 1947 [Taft-Hartley] and from the jurisdiction of the National Labor Relations Board."

The strike in Delano, then, was one in which Cesar Chavez was uncertain of victory. It was also one in which victory, if he did win, could prove in the long run irrelevant. Whatever the strike's outcome, it seemed only a matter of time before mechanization made the farm worker redundant. Over the past fifteen years, the number of farms across the United States has dropped by nearly two million, as larger units, better able to amortize the cost of automation, have absorbed hundreds of thousands of small family farms. The result is that while farms get larger, the farm population has declined sixty percent since 1947, decreasing at the rate of between 100,000 and 200,000 people a year. (Today there are slightly less than two million people who work twenty-five days or more a year in agriculture.) Meanwhile, at the Davis campus of the University of California, and at other institutions concerned with agriculture, scientists and engineers are constantly working on mechanical innovations which ultimately are expected to reduce farm employment to a small cadre of skilled workers.

I was interested in the impact of mechanization, and so one day when I was in Sacramento I made an appointment to see J. E. Becket, a specialist in farm-labor problems at Davis. Once known as the University's "cow college" (its athletic teams are still nicknamed the "Aggies"), Davis had developed, under Clark Kerr, into a liberal-arts school of some distinction, able to attract to its campus such names as William Van O'Connor, Caroline Gordon, and Edgar Friedenberg. It is a pleasant, tree-shaded little town, fifteen miles west of Sacramento, and its streets are lined with large, old white houses with spacious verandas. Though it can hardly be called a hotbed of radicalism, Davis raised far more of a ruckus over Governor Ronald Reagan's proposal to cut the University budget and to make students pay tuition than did its more volatile mother campus at Berkeley.

I saw Mr. Becket in his office, which was so sterile and uncluttered as to be almost modish. Traditionally, he told me, tree crops have been picked by Anglos and stoop crops by Mexicans. Since it is a growers' canon that domestic workers cannot perform stoop labor with anywhere near the efficiency of the Mexicans, I asked him if any productivity studies had been made. "I suppose one reason the growers prefer Mexicans is that they're more easily handled," he said with a trace of a smile. But, in fact, Davis researchers have made a study of the tomato crop and their findings back up the growers' contention. At every age level for both sexes, Mexican nationals were the most productive workers, followed by Mexican-Americans, and last by other domestic workers. I asked if he had an opinion why the Mexicans were more productive. "An opinion only," he said. "The cultural background of the Mexicans makes them more conducive to this kind of work. Their entire environment has been on the farm. And the concept of work is a cultural value to these people. It used to be in this country, but it's a decreasing value today. Leisure is the thing. But to the Mexicans, work is good. There is also the differential in pay, especially for the Mexican nationals. The dollar means much more to them than it does to the domestics. Their idea is to make enough money here to farm their own land down in Mexico. Migrant labor to them is a tremendous opportunity, where it isn't to the domestics."

I asked him about the impact of mechanization on farm labor. "You could have worded that question a little different," he said. "You could have asked 'What is the impact of farm labor on mechanization?' If the labor situation was not as it is, there possibly would be no mechanization. As the labor market becomes scarcer and higher-priced, there naturally is an intensified effort to find a cheaper way to do things. It's a question of which comes first, the chicken or the egg. You can't really say that without the labor shortage there wouldn't be any mechanization, but it has speeded it up. For example, there is right now a practical selective lettuce harvester, but there's such an abundance of labor in lettuce that it's still economically feasible to harvest by hand. The lettuce labor force is almost entirely Mexican. If a completely domestic labor force had to be used, then I think you'd see the machine overnight."

In 1966, Becket said, eighty-five percent of the canned-tomato harvest was done by machine; in wine grapes, an automatic shaker has been developed that will shake the bunches from the vine on to a conveyor belt. "A machine might take fifteen men," he said, "but they're not your traditional farm labor any more. They're skilled hands. And this is your problem. Farming is no longer a status profession. People are moving out of it, not just the field hands, but the farmers, too. If they can find a way out, they will. So what do you do with the Mexican-Americans? Once you teach them English, once you give them a certain level of literacy, do you train them out of agriculture or do you increase their agricultural skills so that they can remain on the farm? I don't know."

Perhaps no state is better suited than California to large-scale agricultural mechanization. Certainly in no other state can agriculture truly be said to be so industrialized. According to the 1959 agricultural census, six percent of California's farms accounted for seventy-five percent of the total farm acreage, while less than fifteen percent accounted for over three quarters of the total production and four fifths of the total farm wages. Though California farmers, when they talk about farming (especially to congressional committees), like to evoke the image of American Gothic, the reality is what Carey McWilliams has called "factories in the field." And it is in the origin and growth of these factories, and the resultant casual exploitation of California farm labor, that the seeds of the Delano grape strike can be found.

The large-scale tilling of the California valleys began in the nascent days of the robber barons, and it was they who seemed to suggest the tone for the evolution of California agriculture. The land, after the war with Mexico, was there for the taking, and the takers were limited only by their own ingenuity. Speed was of the essence. The gold fields were opening up, and as claims failed and dreams of fortune dimmed, the Forty-Niners would be turning to the land for sustenance. Under the terms of the settlement with Mexico, California had been ceded to the United States with the provision that the old Spanish land grants would be respected. There were only some thirty grants under Spanish rule, but on the eve of American occupation, Mexican and American speculators, using all methods of fraud, forgery, and bribery, dredged up hundreds more, with the result that when the United States formally took over California, some eight hundred grants were brought forth consigning over eight million acres of California land to the grantees. The grants, according to McWilliams, whose indispensable book on the bizarre and often tragic history of California agriculture, *Factories in the Field,* is now a collector's item, bringing up to fifteen dollars in some Los Angeles secondhand bookstores, were "amazing items." On the map, one was shaped like a tarantula. Although most were known to be bogus, the majority were upheld by the courts.

The settlement of California brought in the railroads, and they in turn made the fraudulent Mexican land grantees look like novices. By 1870, the railroads held some 20 million acres in rights-of-way; as late as 1919, the Southern Pacific was still the chief landholder in California. Their grants were vague and unpublicized, and often they would let settlers nest on their land, making improvements, and then, once the improvements were made, the railroads would evict them. The federal government in Washington abetted in the looting of the California valleys. Some 3,500,000 acres of "swamp land" were granted to the state, and the speculators immediately moved in, their greed almost beyond belief. "One of them contended that Sierra Valley in Plumas County, in the heart of the Sierra Nevada, was 'swamp' land," McWilliams wrote. "Similarly a beautiful 46,000 acre tract near Sacramento was seized upon as falling into this classification." According to an 1871 report by the State Board of Equalization, a former state Surveyor General left office with 350,000 acres of land, and a former federal Surveyor General with 300,000 acres. By the mid-1870's, reported an editorial in

the Sacramento *Union*, "600 men out of 600,000 own half
the land in this state."

The consolidation of the land into feudal fiefs necessitated a different kind of farm labor. Throughout the rest of
the country, family farms predominated, dependent
mainly on the labor of the farmer and his family. But there
could be no intention that a grower and his kin alone
should tend a holding that, in the case of the Miller and
Lux ranches, exceeded 450,000 acres. Up and down the
California valleys, the "bindle stiff" became a fixture of the
landscape, and around him grew a mystique about migrant labor that prevails even today. "They were
'tramps,'" McWilliams wrote, "shiftless fellows who actually *preferred* 'the open road' and jolly camaraderie of the
tramp jungle to a settled and decent life. There was nothing you could do about these insouciant and lighthearted
boys; you couldn't pay them a decent wage for they
'would drink it up right away.' As for providing them with
shelter or a bed—why, they loved the open air and would
rather die than take a bath." The attitude of the grower
toward the tramps was summed up in a list of written instructions that Henry Miller of Miller and Lux gave his
ranch foremen: "Never refuse a tramp a meal, but never
give him more than one meal. A tramp should be a tramp
and keep on tramping. Never let the tramps eat with the
other men. Make them wait until the men are through,
and then make them eat off the same plates."

By the 1870's, the pattern of California agriculture was
beginning to change, in the nature of both the crop and
the labor force. Where wheat was once the staple crop, it
was giving way to vegetables and deciduous fruit, which
promised a far greater and more stable return. And the

growers were, for the first time, beginning to perceive the benefits of using foreign minorities to work the land. They were more malleable, and because they were for the most part despised foreigners unable to find work in the cities, they could be hired at sub-subsistence wages on the farm. The first great influx of foreign farm labor was Chinese. They had been barred from many of the gold camps (it was the contention of the miners that the Chinese were adept claim and sluice thieves), and with the completion of the transcontinental railroad in 1869, thousands more flooded the labor market. Life in the cities was increasingly unfeasible for them. On a summer evening in 1877, some 300 members of Dennis Kearney's Workingman's Party, after first climbing Nob Hill and demanding that the houses of the Southern Pacific barons be turned over to "the people," went back down the hill and casually burned a few Chinese laundries. Civic ordinances had been passed against the Chinese in San Francisco, and the California Supreme Court had upheld a statute which prohibited the testimony of Chinese, as well as Negroes, mulattos, and Indians, in cases against white men. (In a remarkable example of ethnological reasoning, one justice ruled that a Chinese, in California, was a variety of Indian.) The result of such restrictions was that the Chinese had nowhere to go except to the farms, and so during the 1870's they made up more than seventy-five percent of the farm labor force in the state.

But the tide of resentment against the Chinese was not to be held back, and in 1882 Congress passed, over the frantic lobbying of the California growers, the first Exclusion Act. In the next decade, although their conditions of employment were severely limited by Congress, the Chinese were sorely set upon by white vigilantes. The failure of the banks and the Depression of 1893 threw thousands of whites out of work, and more and more of them took their bitterness out against the Chinese. Mobs razed Chinese labor camps and sacked and looted Chinese business establishments. As they have done for more than a century with every farm minority group, growers maintained they only hired Chinese because they could not pay the wages demanded by domestic workers.

Congress and the vigilantes forced the growers to turn elsewhere for a labor supply. As the Chinese were phased out by fiat and terror, ranchers quietly began to import Japanese to replace them. "The Japanese were regarded as very valuable immigrants," said one state document of the period, "and efforts were made to entice them to come." By the turn of the century, Japanese workers were found in fields and vineyards all over the state. The very shrewdness of the Japanese, however, incurred the antagonism of both the growers and the domestic workers. When they first entered the state, they underbid not only white workers, but Chinese and Hindus as well. They agreed to work for thirty-five and forty cents a day and to provide their own transportation and board. Slowly they began to monopolize farm labor throughout California, and when they had, they started to squeeze the growers for higher wages. "Japanese labor is not cheap labor," wrote a scandalized editorialist for the Los Angeles *Times*. "The little brown traders know how to get as much for their product as the traffic will bear." But what really sharpened the antipathy of the whites was the ambition of the Japanese to hold their own land. "The moment this ambition is exercised," the state Commissioner of Labor Statistics wrote in 1909, "that moment the Japanese ceases to be an ideal laborer." Gradually, the Japanese began to acquire small farms, in the process running up against the hostility of growers who saw their labor supply decreasing and their large units of production threatened. "The Chinese when they were here were ideal," said the proceedings of the California Fruit Growers' Convention of 1907. "They were patient, plodding and uncomplaining in the performance of a most menial service. They submitted to anything, never violating a contract. The Japanese now coming in are a tricky and cunning lot, who break contracts and become quite independent. They are not organized into unions, but their clannishness seems to operate as a union would. One trick is to contract work at a certain price and then in the rush of the harvest season to strike unless wages are raised." Another grower put it more succinctly. "The Japanese is like the Irishman's flea. You think you have him, but you haven't."

The Japanese finally paid the price for their acumen when Congress passed the Immigration Act of 1924, which excluded Japanese from entry into the United States. The growers, however, were not caught short. Hindu workers had begun appearing in California as early as 1907, and the Exclusion Act opened the doors for Mexican immigration. With the various nationalities now in the fields, the growers established different wage scales for different racial groupings, which fostered bitter racial antagonism as the different groups competed for the available jobs. The result, as the growers had foreseen, was that wages were kept at the lowest possible level. The ranchers, however, regarded this ploy as a key to the land of opportunity. "Peon?" asked the *Pacific Rural Press*, commenting on a charge that growers were keeping Mexican nationals in a state of virtual peonage. "Isn't the word peon a little out of character when applied to a Mexican family which buzzes around in its own battered flivver, going from crop to crop, seeing beautiful California, breathing its air, eating its food, and finally doing the homing pigeon stunt back to Mexico with more money than their neighbors dreamed existed?"

The actual feeling of California toward its farm minorities was nowhere near as benign as its public utterances. The publicist for the shipper-growers referred in the *Pacific Rural Press* to the Filipinos, who began to be imported in the early twenties, as "the most worthless, unscrupulous, shiftless, diseased, semi-barbarian that has ever come to our shore." In 1921, a University of California professor published a textbook on farm management in which are reflected the dogmas of ethnically sensitive California: Mexicans were "childish, lazy, unambitious"; Japanese were "tricky and sexually lax"; Hindus were "lean, lanky and enervated"; and Negroes were "notorious prevaricators."

Despite the conditions under which the farm minorities worked, it was not until shortly before World War I that signs of discontent began to be visible in the fields. In 1905, the Industrial Workers of the World was formed in Chicago, and for the next eight years the Wobblies fanned over the country, spreading their creed of agitation on the roads, along the highways, and in the broken-down labor camps. California's migratory labors were a fertile ground for the Wobbly organizers. Essentially migratory themselves, the Wobblies flowed naturally in the currents of farm labor, and the growers were quick to see the threat they posed to the established order. "Hanging is much too good for them and they would be much better dead," the San Diego *Tribune* wrote of the Wobblies in 1912, "for they are absolutely useless in the human economy; they are the waste material of creation and should be drained off into the sewer of oblivion, there to rot in cold obstruction like any other excrement."

But the Wobblies were not to be denied, and in the years before Sarajevo, they set up offices in Fresno, Bakersfield, Los Angeles, San Diego, San Francisco, and Sacramento. Though they had fewer than 5,000 members in California in 1913, and less than eight percent of the migratory laborers were members, their influence was pervasive. The conditions in the camps and the hobo jungles had been fetid for twenty years, and with the arrival of the Wobblies it was only a matter of time before there was militant action. The outbreak took place in the summer of 1913 at the Durst hop ranch in the little town of Wheatland.

The standard of living at the Durst ranch was no better and no worse than at scores of other labor camps all over California. There were some 2,800 men, women, and children gathered there, far more than the harvest called for, since Durst, according to a commission of inquiry set up after the riot, had advertised, in the established grower practice, for more workers than he needed, to keep the wages down. Throughout the season, nearly a thousand people were unable to get work and remained idle. There were Japanese, Hindus, and Puerto Ricans billeted at the camp, as well as white workers from the California towns and cities and drifters from the Sierra foothills, and their wages varied from between seventy-eight cents to a dollar a day. The camp was in such a foul condition that some of the workers, unable to take it any longer, left before the end of the season, thereby forfeiting the ten percent of their wages Durst withheld when they signed on. Tents were rented to the workers at seventy-five cents a week. Many had no blankets and others slept in the open fields. One group of forty-five men, women, and children slept huddled together on a single pile of straw. Dysentery was rampant. There were only nine outdoor toilets for the 2,800 people, creating a stench that hung over the camp like a pall. There was no garbage disposal, no organization for sanitation. Nor was there enough water, which was a boon to Durst's cousin, who had a lemonade concession, selling the juice to the workers at five cents a glass. Local merchants were forbidden to send delivery wagons into the camps, so that the workers would buy their provisions from the company store. Many of the workers who went into the fields were children, and there were numerous instances of children from five to ten years old suffering from sickness and prostration.

Among the strange assemblage at the camp, there were approximately one hundred active or formerly active Wobblies, and on August 3, 1913, they led a mass meeting to protest against their living conditions. One Wobbly organizer, Blackie Ford, took a sick child from its mother's arms and, holding it aloft, shouted, "It's for the kids we are doing this." The demonstrators had just finished singing a Wobbly song when the sheriff arrived with the local district attorney. A deputy fired a shot in the air to quiet the crowd, but the shot had the opposite effect, and a riot started. Some 2,000 campers mixed with the posse, and when order was finally restored, the district attorney, a deputy, and two workers were dead. The state government acted quickly. Four companies of National Guardsmen were dispatched to Wheatland, where they surrounded the camp; all over California, authorities ordered the arrest of Wobblies, whether they had been in Wheatland on August 3 or not. Many of the Wobblies were held incommunicado for weeks, moved from county to county under cover of darkness so that their attorneys could not find them. Eight months after the riot, Blackie Ford and another Wobbly, who was in Arizona when the outbreak occurred, were convicted of murder and sentenced to life in prison.

The effect of Wheatland and the subsequent investigation was to make California dimly aware for the first time of the plight of its migratory workers, but the fear of the Wobblies and of insurrection overcame any but the most primitive attempts at ameliorating their condition. One benevolent grower favored treating workers better by giving them "plenty of clean hay to sleep on," and another described their existence as a refrain from *The Song of the Open Road*. "The fun of the thing," he said, "comes at night when the day's picking is over and supper is done. All the camp gathers together then and the pickers sing and play banjos, and they make love and gossip, and turn in at all hours of the night, always good-natured and jolly and carefree for a season at least."

The onset of World War I put the lid on farm strife. Labor was at a premium and for the next decade growers were pretty much untroubled by unrest in their fields. But their insight about their workers did not improve. Many favored the prohibition amendment as a way to keep their men in line. At a San Francisco symposium, one grower rated the saloon as "a disturbing element" second only to the Wobblies. The closing of the saloons, said a farm journal, "will reduce roadside attractions and facilitate transit as well as insure the greater efficiency of labor upon arrival." It was not until the early thirties that there were any serious attempts to organize the migrants, and this was done without the aid of organized labor, which was too concerned with establishing a beachhead in industry to bother about farm workers. "Only fanatics are willing to live in shacks and tents and get their heads broken in the interests of migratory labor," the AFL's official spokesman in California said in 1935. And so it was left to the Communist Party to take up the cause of the migrants.

In 1931, the Communist-led Cannery and Agricultural Workers' Industrial Union was formed, and for the next two years the CAWIU led strikes in Vacaville, Hayward, Merced, Sacramento, Lodi, Fresno, Gridley, Tulare, and Tagus. The growers formed vigilante groups to combat the strikers, and in Vacaville a masked mob of forty men, according to one observer quoted by Carey McWilliams, "took six strike leaders out of jail, drove them twenty miles from town, flogged them, clipped their heads with sheep clippers, and poured red enamel over them." In Pixley, a union building was riddled with rifle fire, and two workers were killed and several more wounded; eleven ranchers were arrested for murder, but in spite of positive identification, all were acquitted. In the Imperial Valley, local and county police raided the desert camp of the strikers, burning their shacks and driving the 2,000 workers out with tear-gas bombs; one baby was killed in the raid. "The veterans of the Valley," said a past commander of the Valley American Legion Post, "finding that the police agencies were unable to cope with the situation, took matters in their own hands and solved the situation in their own way. Now the Valley is free from all un-American influences." To give a legal veneer to the vigilantism, authorities raided the CAWIU offices in Sacramento on July 20, 1934, and arrested the leaders of the union. Eighteen were placed on trial for violation of the Criminal Syndicalism Law, and on April 1, 1935, eight were convicted and sentenced to prison; their conviction was reversed on appeal two years later, but the CAWIU was for all intents and purposes broken.

As the Depression spread over California, conditions on the farms worsened. In Los Angeles County, one picker worked twenty-nine hours and earned only $1.60; a husband and wife worked in the fields for ten days and made only $9. Though there was not enough work for the California field hands, tens of thousands of destitute refugees from the Dust Bowl poured into the state, brought by glowing promises of immediate employment. In a single November day in 1937, a caravan of 3,000 pea pickers entered the Imperial Valley from Arizona, with as many as thirteen people in one car. The Okies soon settled into a life of almost indescribable wretchedness. "One investigator," McWilliams wrote, "reported that he had found a two-room cabin in which forty-one people from southern Oklahoma were living; another described a one-room shack in which fifteen men, women, and children, 'festering sores of humanity,' lived in 'unimaginable filth.' One ranch provided a single bathhouse and a single shower in connection with a block of houses capable of housing 400 people. Most of the boasted model camps maintained by the growers were found to be without baths, showers, or plumbing. In most districts, the workers bathed and drank from irrigation ditches. Eighteen families were found living in Kingsburg, under a bridge. Workers in large numbers were found living in shacks built of linoleum and cardboard cartons; in tents improvised of gunny sacks on canal banks with coffee cans serving for chimneys on their makeshift stoves. In some cases, bits of carpet or sacking had been tacked against a tree for shelter. Health and sanitary conditions were found to be equally appalling. Fifty babies, the children of migratory workers, died of diarrhea and enteritis in one county in a single season. In one ditch camp, twenty-seven out of thirty children were found to be defective through malnutritional diseases."

This was the way of life John Steinbeck laid bare in *The Grapes of Wrath* and *In Dubious Battle* and which Mc-Williams himself exposed at the end of the thirties. In some slight way, they managed to prick the public conscience, and there were fumbling efforts at redress. But once again, before pressure could be brought on the growers, war intervened. After the Japanese attack on Pearl Harbor, manpower was drained from the fields into the military and into the war plants. The shortage was made more acute in 1942 by the relocation of Japanese-Americans into detention compounds for the duration of World War II. In desperate need of labor, growers prevailed upon Congress to enter into an informal agreement with Mexico to provide the necessary workers. In the eyes of the growers, these workers, or *braceros,* were an ideal commodity. They were imported only for the duration of the season and could be sent home at the end of the harvest, which prevented them from heeding the siren call of the shipyards. On August 4, 1942, the first informal agreement was signed between Mexico and the United States, and for the next twenty-two years the *braceros* formed the backbone of California labor.

Until 1951, the *braceros* came into the United States under the informal arrangement with the Mexican government. But there were so many abuses in the program that Mexico, early that year, let Washington know that the informal agreements were no longer acceptable. Contracting thereafter must come under the supervision of a United States government agency. Too many growers had reneged on wage payments and transportation back to Mexico, and the *braceros* themselves brought back tales of wanton discrimination throughout California and the Southwest. (At one time, over fifty counties in Texas were on a proscribed list maintained by the Mexican government.) Moreover, growers were undercutting the *bracero* program through the wholesale employment of illegal wetback labor, which slipped across the border, often with the connivance of the Border Patrol, and fanned into the farms and vineyards. Before the tide was stemmed, in the middle fifties, as many as one million illegal laborers were caught and deported back to Mexico in a given year. Growers said that they did not know who was legal and who was not. "We only accept a man's word for it," Robert DiGiorgio of the huge DiGiorgio agricultural combine told a congressional committee in 1949. But there was scarcely a grower who did not know a labor contractor who would supply illegal seasonal help. No embarrassing questions were asked; no embarrassing answers given. The advantage of the wetbacks was obvious. They were not contract labor bound to a single employer, like the *braceros,* and could thus move freely through the state.

They could be employed at a cut-rate wage, and because of their illegal status they could not complain if they were cheated. More than one grower would inform the Border Service at the end of a season that there were illegals on his ranch, in the hope that immediate deportation of the workers would save him the need of paying their wages.

On July 12, 1951, therefore, Congress formalized the *bracero* program by passing Public Law 78, which regulated the flow of imported labor into the United States. The most important provision of P.L. 78 was that no *braceros* could be employed where domestic labor was available. But the growers used every possible ruse to get around this provision, and in many cases they found a valuable ally in the rancher-oriented Farm Placement Service. Domestic workers were told that a ranch was not hiring, when obviously there was work available, or they were offered one wage by the Farm Placement Service and a lower wage by the grower when they arrived in the fields. In one town, the Farm Placement Service advised asparagus cutters that the black peat land was an irritant to fair-skinned people. Workers dependent on a single automobile to get to work were sent to different farms so that those without a car were without transportation and hence without a job. Growers neglected to give domestics notice of transfer to other fields, so that when they finally arrived on the job they found that they had been replaced by *braceros*. So great was the harassment, so slim the chances of employment, that thousands of domestic workers simply stopped seeking farm work, leading growers to contend even more vigorously that domestics would not do stoop labor. In the fields, the number of *braceros* multiplied until, in the early sixties, nearly 300,000 were employed in the harvest. Though they were making far more money, at the expense of the domestics, than they ever could have in Mexico, their lot was not an easy one. Their camps were mosquito-infested and often they were billeted in skimpily reconverted barns and stables. The buses and trucks used by the growers to transport the *braceros* to and from the fields were often so dilapidated that they were the cause of tragic roadside accidents: eight dead in Brawley in 1953 when a truck with defective brakes piled into a locomotive; thirty-two hospitalized in Stanislaus County in 1957 when a produce truck with neither seats nor overhead cover overturned; fourteen burned to death in Soledad in 1958 when a truck caught fire from spilled gasoline.

It was not until the early sixties that pressure began to build in Congress to let P.L. 78 lapse. What swung the pendulum was concern not so much for the farm workers as over the gold outflow. Nearly every cent the *braceros* made went back to Mexico, draining upwards of $100 million in gold out of the United States annually at a time when the country could ill afford to lose it. As Congress began to waver, the California growers put up a spirited fight to save P.L. 78. Their arguments were the traditional ones: Anglos would not do stoop labor; without the *braceros,* California agriculture would collapse; the collapse of California agriculture meant the collapse of the nation. Nor were the growers without concern for the economy of Mexico, fretting that the end of P.L. 78 would spell starvation for thousands of families across the border. It was a touching venture into free-market economics, since most growers are high-tariff, against foreign aid, and would not buy a foreign car or fly a foreign airline.

With attendant attention from the press, growers in Orange and Monterey counties plowed under rows of their fields, dramatically stating that they would rather do this than see their crop rot as it inevitably would without the *braceros*. But the growers were met head on by the clergy, liberals, and elements of organized labor tuned to the sad situation of farm labor. "I have no tears to waste on those who have been crying disaster at the prospect of losing the previously available agricultural workers from Mexico under P.L. 78, but who in the meantime have taken no realistic steps to secure an adequate and dependable United States labor force," Father James L. Vizzard, S.J., of the National Catholic Rural Life Conference told a labor hearing in 1964. "Since these growers show no signs of self-reform, they need to be told emphatically and with finality that the approximation of slave labor conditions which they have perpetuated will no longer be tolerated by this nation. They need to be made to understand in what century and in what kind of economy and society they are living and operating. They must be forced to realize that to exploit the poverty of other nations in order to beat down and crush the poor of our own country is the grossest kind of immorality."

The rhetoric of Father Vizzard and other men of like mind stiffened Congressional supporters of the farm workers, and on December 31, 1964, P.L. 78, the *bracero* law, expired and passed into history. (Over a year later, I received a telephone call from a total stranger in Brownsville, Texas, who had read of my interest in farm labor. He was in Brownsville, he informed me, on a tour of border towns to assess the social havoc caused by the end of the *bracero* program. It was his contention that Congress, by letting P.L. 78 lapse, was directly responsible for an increase in prostitution along the border among young women who might otherwise be more profitably and morally employed picking crops in California. He did not cite the source of his statistics.)

The end of the *bracero* program stabilized California's labor force for the first time in years. No longer could growers drain off the south-of-the-border labor pool that kept domestic wages depressed and, because of the threat that Mexican nationals would take over the available jobs, discouraged agricultural unrest. But the lapsing of P.L. 78 was only one of a combination of circumstances far from Delano that conspired to make the time for a strike propitious. Civil-rights agitation in the South had stirred eddies of guilt in the nation's psyche about its economically and culturally dispossessed, and as the ripples widened, they naturally began to take in California's Mexican-American minority. And then the United States Supreme Court, in its one-man, one-vote reapportionment decisions, effectively demolished rural domination of the state legislatures. Reapportionment in California meant that half of the forty state senators would come from south of the Tehachapis in the urban sprawl of Southern California. "Getting rid of the cows-and-acres senators is important," I was told one day by Paul Schrade, the director of the United Auto Workers' Region 6 and one of Chavez's earliest and most vociferous boosters. "Most of the union and minority strength is in the cities. They can exert the kind of pressure that urban senators are susceptible to. So now it's possible to envision the kind of legislation that can really benefit farm labor, like the collective-bargaining rights industrial workers have."

None of these elements, however, would have mattered without the man to take advantage of them, and none of these elements created that man. In the past, too many factors militated against a successful organizing campaign among farm workers. The work was seasonal, the work force migratory, and with such a short-term employer-employee relationship, the organizers could never generate any real leverage against the growers. Matters were complicated by the fact that the Mexican-Americans did not really trust Anglo labor organizers. They suspected that labor's agents were trying to lure them into unions only to collect their dues and help industrial unions, many of which had notoriously discriminated against Latins. For years, in fact, the big unions had sold out farm labor. Farm labor benefits tacked onto state and federal legislations were invariably compromised away to gain additional advantages for organized industrial workers. Indifference on the part of the unorganized Mexican-Americans paralysed the AFL-CIO when, in the 1950's, it finally set up the Agricultural Workers Organizing Committee. Nor did AWOC help itself by its reliance upon traditional trade-union organizing techniques. Rather than working directly with the field hands, AWOC went through the labor contractors who hire the field workers and then lease them to the growers. In some instances, the contractors would not let the workers board the bus to the fields until they had come up with their dues. Such tactics hardly encouraged any abiding faith in the union, and finally, after seven fruitless years and a million dollars spent, the AFL-CIO downgraded AWOC to a token effort with enough funds to maintain an office in Stockton and little more. What the farm workers clearly lacked was indigenous Mexican-American leadership. Not only the unions, but also the liberals, radicals, and socialists desperately interested in their plight were unable to rally them into action. "We were leaders without followers," recalls writer Paul Jacobs, one of the founders of Citizens for Farm Labor, an organization dedicated to improving the conditions of the farm workers. "When we appeared at meetings to protest the use of *braceros*, we had to import farm workers to give body to our group. We spoke on behalf of the farm workers, but all we could do was make a loud noise, based on our status as 'dignitaries' in the community."

Late in the 1950's, however, political seismographers began to detect rumblings of discontent within the Mexican-American community. The sharpest tremors could be traced to the Community Service Organization, a group headed by Saul Alinsky, the self-styled "professional radical" who had spent years mobilizing ghettoes across the United States. It was Alinsky's theory that the poor, in this case the Mexican-Americans, already had by the sheer force of their numbers the primary instrument to effect social change. Because Cesar Chavez had been trained by Alinsky in the CSO, I arranged to visit Alinsky one day in Carmel, California, to see how the CSO had applied his tenets. He is a bespectacled, squarely built man in his late fifties, with a weary, ironic voice. His conversation is littered with Anglo-Saxonisms and he appears totally without illusions. "Wherever I go there's trouble," he said as he stirred a Scotch on the rocks with his finger. "I've always said that the only way to talk to the Establishment is not through their ears but through their rears. You've got to shaft them up the ass. Liberals would never talk like that. The trouble with liberals is that they think that a guy's got to be ninety percent on the side of the angels. I say you get a guy who's fifty point oh-oh-oh-oh one percent good, you got a goddam saint."

He paused for a moment. We were sitting in the bar of the Hotel La Playa and there was a wedding going on in the dining room. "The thing about this racket," he said after the nuptial rice was thrown, "is that no one has a sense of humor. I was in Detroit at a meeting with Stokely Carmichael, and some minister asked him if he had anything good to say about the United States. So Stokely reaches for his suitcase and I said to myself, 'Oh, Jesus, any time Stokely goes for that suitcase, you know he's going to haul out a book, as if some crummy book is the last word on any given subject.' Well, he gets this book and begins reading John Donne's 'No Man Is an Island,' for Christ's sake. When he finishes, he says, '*That* is my answer.' I couldn't look. I was holding my head in my hands. Later I said to him, 'Stokely, why didn't you read *The Cremation of Sam McGee?*' I think he would have done it, so I had to go back to him and tell him not to or he would have started looking around to see what Robert W. Service had to say about Black Power."

Alinsky blueprinted his tactics in a book published some twenty years ago called *Reveille for Radicals.* "A democracy lacking in popular participation dies of paralysis," he wrote then, and to increase the popular participation he designed a series of militant "People's Organizations." Their tools were sit-downs, boycotts, strikes, demonstrations, mass meetings, and picket lines. "What happens when we come in?" he asked in a series of taped interviews for *Harper's Magazine.* "We say, 'Look, you don't have to take this. There is something you can do about it. But you have to have power to do it, and you'll only get it through organization. Because power just goes to two poles—to those who've got money and those who've got people. You haven't got money, so your own fellow men are your only source of strength. Now the minute you can do something about it, you've got a problem. Should I handle it this way or that way? You're active. And all of a sudden you stand up.'"

Alinsky said that these were the tactics he used with the CSO. "To get something like the CSO going," he said, "you've got to pick issues that will build your army, not real issues that depend on winning or losing. You zero in on somebody, give him the business, some liberal thinker on the board of education, say, who says he's on your side, but isn't doing anything about it. You let him have it, get him mad, make him say something that he'll regret that will bring people over to your side. As a result of the reaction, you bring in recruits. The action is the reaction."

Recruits without organization, however, are meaningless. "That's the basic plague of the civil-rights struggle," he said. "No one can distinguish between a movement and an organization. You have a march and a lot of speeches, then it pisses out—that's a movement. It's the old story. The operation was a success, but the patient died. An organization keeps on growing, keeps on making trouble, keeps on chipping away to get what it wants. The trouble with liberals is that they've all got a third-act mentality. They want everything all wrapped up in a big goddam box; then—curtain. They want to skip the first two acts, all the tediousness of organizing. It doesn't work that way.

If you want drama, get a movement; if you want results, you've got to have an organization."

The impetus to the CSO came, more or less, as the result of a poker game. Playing cards one night, Alinsky heard that the American Council of Race Relations was going to fire one of its officials, Fred Ross. "The complaint about Ross was that he was always organizing," Alinsky recalls. "Right away my ears pricked up at this and so I hired him." A tall, quiet man with a seamed, sad face, Ross would be perfectly cast for the role of Jesus Christ in a Passion play. He roamed the Valley for the CSO, needling the Mexicans into political awareness, and when he had formed a nucleus of workers willing to carry on the CSO's work in one town, he would move on to the next. Through the CSO, the Mexican-Americans began to take action, first on such bread and butter items as better sewage disposal and new sidewalks, and then through the ballot box with bloc voting, thus impressing on local political candidates that the Mexican-Americans could no longer be overlooked. It was for the CSO that Ross first recruited Cesar Chavez and in the CSO that Chavez matured, distilling his belief that farm workers should be organized and that this organization would have to come from within. At last the time and the circumstances had met the man.

FIVE

I was in Delano for ten days before I could pin Chavez down for any appreciable time. He is constantly on the move, and virtually the only way to spend any time with him is to volunteer to be his chauffeur. He seems to transact most of his business in Delano from the back of a car, going from his own office at 102 Albany to the other buildings on the West Side into which the burgeoning NFWA staff has overflowed and which are identified simply by their colors—the Pink House and the Gray House. He is a short man, thirty-eight when the strike started, growing heavy around the middle, with a dark walnut complexion, coal-black hair, and restless dark eyes. In the normal sense of the word, Chavez is almost impossible to interview. In the first place, he is just short of pathologically suspicious of Anglos, even some of those most closely connected with the NFWA. (One of his staunchest supporters told me that once when he tried to press some advice on Chavez, which in retrospect proved quite sound, he was rebuffed with the words, "You'll never understand, you're an Anglo." The friend said that Chavez was immediately embarrassed and apologized, but still resisted the counsel.) Secondly, so many reporters have come to Delano since the strike started, all asking the same questions, that by now Chavez gives his answers almost by rote, honing them to the point where one is impressed more by their pithiness than by their content. It is hard to tax him for this, as the ignorance about the strike on the part of some of the visiting press would have tried the patience of Job. While I was in Delano, a reporter-photographer team from a national magazine arrived for the standard overnight visit. The photographer was surprised to learn that he was in the San Joaquin Valley, which he had thought was in the state of Washington, and the reporter, in the words of one observer, "wouldn't know a grape if he saw one in the Safeway." I saw them the following morning at 102 Albany trying to hire a picket line for a photograph, advising the NFWA magnanimously to "send the bill for the gas to New York."

When Chavez loosens up, however, he is both articulate and humorous. The Messianic quality about him is suggested by his voice, which is mesmerizing—soft, perfectly modulated, pleasantly accented. More than anything else, he seems to impart what Fred Ross calls "a sense of quiet power." He is infinitely patient, and deferential almost to a fault. "Cesar hates to give orders," one of his supporters says. "When you are driving with him and he is giving directions, he never says 'Turn here, go there.' He says 'Now we turn here, now let's stop there.' " Despite the demands on his time, he will stop and listen to the most mundane problems of any striker. One day when I was driving him around, he was running far behind schedule as he tried to get depositions from a number of fired workers before they left town. Yet he still paused at the camp the NFWA maintains on the outskirts of Delano, to talk to a mechanic about the paucity of spare parts for the union's automobiles, then concerned himself with trying to fix a leaky hose. At 2 a.m. that same morning, a carload of food for the strikers had arrived in front of his house. Rather than give the driver directions to the storehouse at the camp, which is difficult to find in the dark, he got out of bed and drove out there with him and helped unload the truck himself.

There is nothing of the bombastic Latin politician about Chavez. His words are edged only by the softest irony. "The idea still prevails," he told me one day with a slight, resigned smile, "that farmworkers are a different breed of people—humble, happy, built close to the ground." It was to correct this impression, to give dignity to the farm worker, that the strike began. "Some people say, write off this generation of parents and hope my son gets out of farm work," he told the Senate Subcommittee on Migratory Labor. "Well, I'm not ready to be written off as a loss, and farm work could be a decent job for my son, with a union. But the point is that this generation of farm labor children will not get an adequate education until their parents earn enough to care for the child the way they want to and the way other children in school—the ones who succeed—are cared for.

"The average farm worker in Delano has seven children, lives in a house which he rents for $55 a month, makes payments on a car, furniture, and to a finance company. Before the strike, he worked eight months of the year at $1.10 an hour, and his wife worked four months beside him. On weekends and in the summer, his children worked too. This average farm worker buys food at the same stores at the same prices as the rancher does. And he's not making it. So now these average workers are strikers; they've been willing to lose their cars, furniture, to live on beans and more beans, to work 'on the line' seventy hours a week for the right to a living wage."

What constitutes a living wage is a matter of lively debate in Delano. It is virtually impossible to talk to a grower without having him pull out his daily tally sheets to show that his workers—with their piece rates—average $1.78, $1.93, $2.14 an hour. "My men would be losing money if they went into Chavez's union," Jack Pandol, a local grower, told me with some exasperation one day. "What kind of union is it that guarantees $1.40 when my men are making $1.78?" There was a kind of engaging perversity about the question, which was often asked by growers and which suggested that Chavez was trying to impose a ceiling rather than a minimum wage, with no allowance for incentive rates. "They think people live by the hour and not by the year," Chavez said when I told him about the conversation. "They say the farm workers are happy living the way they are—just like the Southern plantation owner used to say about his Negroes."

This innuendo of racial discrimination creeps into every strike discussion on the West Side. NFWA adherents claim that it is impossible for a Mexican to buy property on the East Side, that more Mexicans than Anglos are expelled from the local high school for the same offenses, that the police docket is overloaded with cases against Mexicans and Filipinos. The spirit of these claims is vigorously disputed on the other side of Highway 99. I was shown reams of statistics to prove that the NFWA was engaging in the worst kind of slander against Delano. It was unfailingly pointed out to me that Chavez himself lived on the East Side, that the chairman of the Delano Planning Commission was a Mexican and the president of the elementary school board a Japanese. One charge that I could check . out myself was the claim that the Delano cemetery was rigidly segregated, with the Mexicans and Filipinos all interred in one section and the Anglos in the other. I spent the better part of a morning walking through the cemetery row by row, checking the names on the headstones, and discovered that, like every statement of fact in Delano, this was an ambiguous truth. There was an occasional Mexican grave scattered among the Anglos, an occasional Anglo name (which might have been, I was told, that of a Negro) among the Mexicans.

Discrimination in Delano, as in all the Valley towns, is far more subtle than police charge sheets and segregated cemeteries. "The most overt manifestation of it," one troubled East Sider whose sympathies lay reluctantly with the growers told me, "is the way the ranchers underestimated Chavez. They thought he was just another dumb Mex." Far more pervasive is the acceptance of the way the itinerant Mexicans are forced to live; or perhaps it is more accurate to say the disinclination even to think about it. This disinclination does not mask any deeply suppressed guilt, as outlanders are prone to assume, but is simply regarded as a fact of life in the Valley. One afternoon I drove out of Delano to one Valley fact of life, the notorious Linnell Labor Camp maintained by the Tulare County Housing Authority. There are two types of family housing in the camp. The first is for foremen and labor contractors, who live in relatively comfortable apartments. The housing for the field workers was altogether different. These are no more than sheet-metal tents, approximately eight by fourteen feet, and house a man and wife and up to four children. There is no heat, other than a bottled-gas cooking stove, and no running water in the huts. One tenant said that each unit was a refrigerator in the winter and an oven in the summer. The summers, he said, were the worst. When it was cold, families could pile more blankets on the beds and huddle together, but in the summer the only escape from the heat was to evacuate the shanties. When the workers returned from the fields, they and their families remained outside until the sun went down. Only then did the metal shacks cool off sufficiently to allow the wife to cook dinner. Constructed in the thirties, the units have been officially condemned as unfit for human habitation, but as no replacements were available, they were still occupied.

After my first trip to Delano in the summer of 1966, I checked with the Industrial Union Department of the AFL-CIO and discovered that such conditions as exist in the Linnell Camp have relegated the Mexicans in the Valley to an even lower social position than California's Negroes. Though not by much, their average income and educational achievement are lower. Farm labor families are also more susceptible to chronic ill health. In a 1960 state survey of one hundred agricultural families in Fresno County (half of whom were Mexican-American), it was discovered that fifty-nine percent of the children under three years old had not received immunizations against diphtheria, whooping cough, lockjaw, or smallpox; fifty-eight percent of those under eighteen had not been immunized against polio. Less than half the families interviewed had a water tap in their homes. Seven families had to haul water, and the remainder used community taps located outside their dwellings. Two thirds of the families had no private flush toilets; less than one third had community flush toilets. About a quarter had private privies, while six families used community privies. More than half the people interviewed lived two or three persons to a room;

twenty-two families slept four or more to a room. A quarter of the families had no means of refrigerating their food.

In Valley schools, these *barrio* conditions have engendered subliminal humiliations. In a 1966 Stanford University doctoral thesis, Theodore W. Parsons, who spent forty days observing classes in a Valley elementary school where the student body was fifty-eight percent Mexican, cited some examples. One teacher, asked why she had called on an Anglo boy to lead five Mexicans in orderly file out of the classroom, replied, "His father owns one of the big farms in the area and one day he will have to know how to handle Mexicans." Another teacher, following the general practice of calling on Anglos to help Mexican pupils recite in class, said in praise of the system, "It draws them [the Anglos] out and gives them a feeling of importance." Praising the school principal, the president of the local Chamber of Commerce declared, "He runs a good school. We never have any trouble in our school. Every kid knows his place. We believe that every kid has to learn to respect authority and his betters." And the principal said, "Once we let a Mexican girl give a little talk of some kind and all she did was mumble around. She had quite an accent too. Afterwards we had several complaints from parents, so we haven't done anything like that since. That was about twelve years ago."

SIX

Cesar Estrada Chavez was a *barrio* baby. He was born in Yuma, Arizona, into a family of five children whose father scratched out a precarious existence on a small farm near the Colorado River. His father went broke when Cesar was ten years old, and the family began trailing the crops from Arizona to California and back. Home was a succession of labor camps or the back of a ramshackle automobile. The time was the Depression and there were more workers than there was work. Labor contractors papered the Dust Bowl with the promise of employment, and regiments of Okies swept into California like tumbleweed, only to discover that they were too many and too late. School was something to be fitted in whenever the opportunity presented itself. To this day, Chavez cannot remember how many schools he went to; the number escalates from thirty-one to sixty-seven, although this last is probably the total number he and his brothers and sisters together attended. It was an education that was to leave a lasting mark.

"Those early days when we first came to California were rough," Chavez recalled in a series of interviews for the Farm Worker Press, a subsidiary of the NFWA set up to publicize the plight of the *campesinos* (farm workers). "We were really green, and whenever a labor contractor told us something, we fell for it hook, line, and sinker. We didn't know the ropes yet and got hooked every time. I remember the first year we ended up in the fall picking wine grapes for a contractor near Fresno. They were bad grapes, there were very few bunches on the vines, and we were the only family working in the field. But we were too green to wonder why we were the only ones, you see. After the first week of work, my father asked the contractor for his pay. 'I can't pay you because I haven't been paid by the winery,' the contractor told my father. But we were broke, absolutely broke, with nothing at all to eat, so the contractor finally gave us twenty dollars and said we'd get a big check later when the winery paid him. We worked for seven weeks like that, and each payday the contractor said he couldn't pay us because the winery hadn't paid him yet. At the end of the seventh week, we went to the contractor's house and it was empty. He owed us for seven weeks' pay and we haven't seen him to this day.

"We were desperate. We ran into another labor contractor in Fresno. 'There's lots of money in the cotton near Mendota,' he told us. It was late November by now and it was cold and raining almost every day. Because of the rain, there was almost no work at all. Well, we finally learned the ropes. We learned where the crops were and when they needed workers and we learned little tricks like living under bridges and things like that. Once we learned the ropes, we began helping other green families like we had been, so they wouldn't have it as rough as we did. About 1939, we were living in San Jose. One of the old CIO unions began organizing workers in the dried-fruit industry, so my father and uncle became members. Sometimes the men would meet at our house and I remember seeing their picket signs and hearing them talk. They had a strike and my father and uncle picketed at night. It made a deep impression on me. But of course they lost the strike, and that was the end of the union. But from that time on, my father joined every new agricultural union that came along—often he was the first one to join—and when I was nineteen, I joined the National Agricultural Workers' Union. But it didn't have any more success than any of the other farm workers' unions."

In time, Chavez left home and began to follow the crops on his own. One of his stops was in Delano, where he met and married his wife, Helen. It was at this time that he had his first brush with the Delano establishment. He and Helen were sitting in a movie one night when an usherette asked them to move. Chavez refused and the usherette called the manager, who in turn called the police. Under duress, Chavez was taken from his seat and escorted to the police station, where he was charged with violating the theater's seating policy—Mexicans on one side of the aisle, Anglos on the other.

Chavez's odyssey finally took him back to San Jose, where he went to work in the apricot orchards. At this juncture, in 1952, fate stepped into his life in the person of Fred Ross of the Community Service Organization. Of all the people who have attached themselves to Chavez, Ross is by far the most impressive. I talked to him about his early days with Chavez one afternoon in the coffee shop of the Stardust Motel. "Cesar was living in an area called *Sal Si Puedes,* which means 'Get Out If You Can,'" Ross said. "It was a tough slum with a high proportion of San Quentin alumni. I was trying to organize CSO chapters, and Helen Chavez's name had been given to me by a

Mexican-American public-health nurse. Cesar wasn't at home the first several times I called, but on the fourth time he had about thirty people in the house and I could see that they were going to give this *gringo* a hard time. I could almost hear them thinking, 'What's he know about our problems?' At first they were very hostile when I started to tell them about the CSO. But then they began recognizing certain names and certain incidents like 'Bloody Christmas.'" (This was an incident in which seven Mexicans were beaten up one Christmas Eve by drunken police officers at the Lincoln Heights police station in Los Angeles. The CSO took on their case and after a continual protest got the police department to investigate. As a result, six police officers were sent to jail for from one to ten years.)

"Well, they'd all heard about 'Bloody Christmas,'" Ross continued, "and that got them interested. Now, instead of refusing my cigarettes when I passed them around, they began to accept them. No one there was more enthusiastic than Cesar. I was keeping a diary in those days, and that night when I got home I wrote in it, 'I think I've found the guy I'm looking for.' You could tell it even then."

Chavez became chairman of the CSO's voter-registration drive and in a period of two months he registered over 4,000 people. "It was the first time there had ever been a voter-registration drive among the Mexican-Americans," Ross said, "and the local Republicans were plenty worked up. They announced they were going to have challengers at the voting places because the CSO was registering *braceros* and dead people. So we had our own challengers at the polls to challenge the Anglos. Pretty soon the literacy-test line was longer than the voting line."

After the election, Chavez was laid off his job, but he got hold of an office and went to work helping Mexicans obtain their citizenship. It was the first time such an organized program had been set up, and in the next eight years it helped some 30,000 Mexicans get their papers. At the beginning, Chavez was out of a job, living on unemployment, but Ross finally got Saul Alinsky to hire him as a paid staffer for the CSO at a salary of $325 a month. "It was pretty tough for me at first," Chavez recalled in another interview, taped for *Ramparts* magazine. "I was changing and I had to take a lot of ridicule from the kids my age, the rough characters I worked with in the fields. They would say, 'Hey, big shot, now that you're a politico, why are you working here for sixty-five cents an hour?' After six months of working every night in San Jose, Fred assigned me to take over the CSO chapter in Decoto. It was a tough spot to fill. I would suggest something and people would say, 'No, let's wait until Fred gets back,' or 'Fred wouldn't do it that way.' This is pretty much a pattern with people, I discovered, whether I was put in Fred's position, or later, when someone else was put in my position. After the Decoto assignment, I was sent to start a new chapter in Oakland. Before I left, Fred came to a place in San Jose called the Hole-in-the-Wall and we talked for half an hour over coffee. He was in a rush to leave, but I wanted to keep him talking. I was that scared of my assignment.

"These were hard times in Oakland. First of all, it was a big city and I'd get lost every time I went anywhere. Then I arranged a series of house meetings. I would get to the meeting early and drive back and forth past the house, too nervous to go in and face the people. Finally I would force myself to go inside and sit in a corner. I was quite thin then, and young, and most of the people were middle-aged. Someone would say, 'Where's the organizer?' And I would pipe up, 'Here I am.' Then they would say in Spanish—these were very poor people and we hardly spoke anything but Spanish—'Ha, this *kid?*' Most of them said they were interested, but the hardest part was to get them to start pushing themselves, on their own initiative.

"The idea was to set up a meeting and then get each attending person to call his own house meeting, inviting new people—a sort of chain-letter effect. After a house meeting, I would lie awake going over the whole thing, playing the tape back, trying to see why people laughed at one point, or why they were for one thing and against another. I was also learning to read and write those late evenings. I had left school in the seventh grade and my reading wasn't the best.

"After four months in Oakland, I was transferred. The chapter was beginning to move on its own, so Fred assigned me to organize the San Joaquin Valley. Over the months, I developed what I used to call schemes or tricks —now I call them techniques—of making initial contacts. The main thing in convincing someone is to spend some time with him. It doesn't matter if he can read, write, or even speak well. What is important is that he is a man, and second, that he has shown some initial interest. One good way to develop leadership is to take a man with you in your car. And it works a lot better if you are doing the driving. That way, you are in charge. You drive, he sits there, and you talk. These little things were very important to me. I was caught in a big game by then, figuring out what makes people work. I found out that if you work hard enough, you can usually shake people into working too, those who are concerned. You work harder, and they work harder still, up to a point, and then they pass you. Then, of course, they're on their own."

Chavez ranged over the Valley, setting up new chapters in Madera, Bakersfield, and Hanford. "That was during the McCarthy era and there was a great deal of opposition," Ross told me. "In every town, people were calling us Reds and pointing the finger at Alinsky, who they were convinced was a Communist." To gain new members more rapidly, Chavez set up a service program to deal with the most basic bread-and-butter problems. He got Mexicans out of jail, inquired about their welfare payments, helped them get driver's licenses, settled their immigration status with the proper authorities. "One of his big things was trying to get people who were in trouble with the law not to plead guilty because they had no money to hire an attorney," Ross said. "He scrounged around and got them lawyers, and when they were acquitted, a lot of them were tied up to him for good in gratitude."

During this period, Chavez's ideas were beginning to jell. "I learned to keep away from the established groups and so-called leaders, and to guard against philosophizing," he says. "Working with low-income people is a lot different from working with professionals, who like to sit around talking about how to play politics. When you're trying to recruit a farm worker, you have to paint a little picture, and then you have to color the picture in. We found out that the harder a guy is to convince, the better leader or member he becomes. When you exert yourself to convince him, you have his confidence and he has good motivation. A lot of people who say okay right away wind up hanging around the office, taking up the workers' time.

"And I learned quickly that there is no real appreciation. Whatever you do, and no matter what reasons you may give to others, you do it because you want to see it done, or maybe because you want power. And there shouldn't be any appreciation, understandably. I know good organizers who were destroyed, washed out, because they expected people to appreciate what they'd done. Anyone who comes in with the idea that farm workers are free of sin and that the growers are all bastards either has never dealt with the situation or is an idealist of the first order. Things don't work that way."

Chavez worked for the CSO for ten years, becoming in 1958 general director of the entire national organization. But the very success of the CSO had within it the seeds of Chavez's dissatisfaction. He felt that the CSO was veering too far from its radical origins, that it was attracting too many middle-class professional people—doctors, lawyers, politicians, more interested in the prestige of the organization than in the urgent task of mobilizing the poor. His own interest had begun to focus entirely on the CSO's supporting a movement to organize farm workers, but it was a plan the urban professionals found too parochial. To show his displeasure at what he considered the emasculation of the CSO, Chavez began to appear at meetings coatless and tieless and ultimately refused even to shave or cut his hair. Finally, in 1962, after his farm-union proposal was voted down at the CSO convention, Chavez resigned from the organization. Even a rich member's last minute offer of $50,000 to carry through his plan could not make him reconsider his resignation. "He thought there would be too many strings attached," Ross said, "too many people telling him what to do. And besides, he has this theory that having money is no way to organize. He thinks people will work harder if there's no big money around. And that the people being organized will be a lot more susceptible when they see the organizers aren't a lot better off than they are."

It was only natural that Chavez should return to Delano and with his $1,200 savings start the National Farm Workers' Association. "Helen came from here," he told me one day, "and I knew that no matter what happened, I would always have a roof over my head, a place to get a meal." Methodically he canvassed the Valley, trying to find a nucleus of supporters in each town. "By hand, I drew a map of all the towns between Arvin and Stockton —eighty-six of them, including farming camps—and decided to hit them all," he recalls. "For six months I traveled around, planting an idea. We had a simple questionnaire, a little card with space for name, address, and how much the worker thought he ought to be paid. My wife mimeographed them and we took our kids for two- or three-day jaunts to these towns, distributing the cards door-to-door and to camps and groceries.

"Some 80,000 cards were sent back from eight Valley counties. I got a lot of contacts that way, but I was shocked at the wages the people were asking. "The growers were paying a dollar and $1.15, and maybe ninety-five percent of the people thought they should be getting only $1.25 an hour. Some people scribbled messages on the cards: 'I hope to God we win' or 'Do you think we can win?' or 'I'd like to know more.' So I separated the cards with penciled notes, got in my car, and went to those people. We didn't have any money at all, none for gas and hardly any for food. So I started asking for food. It turned out to be about the best thing I could have done, although at first it's hard on your pride. Some of our best members came in that way. If people give you their food, they'll give you their hearts."

Whenever she could, Helen Chavez worked in the fields, and when funds got particularly low, Chavez took Sunday jobs digging ditches. "Once we were facing a $180 gas bill on a credit card I'd got a long time ago and was about to lose," Chavez says. "And we *had* to keep that credit card. One day my wife and I were picking cotton, pulling bolls to make a little money to live on. Helen said to me, 'Do you put all this in the bag, or just the cotton?' I thought she was kidding and told her to throw the whole boll in so that she had nothing but a sack of bolls at the weighing. The man said, 'Whose sack is this?' I said, 'Well, my wife's,' and he told us we were fired. 'Look at all that crap you brought in,' he said. Helen and I started laughing. We were going anyway. We took the four dollars we had earned and spent it at a grocery store where they were giving away a $100 prize. Each time you shopped, they'd give you one of the letters of M-O-N-E-Y or a flag. You had to have M-O-N-E-Y plus the flag to win. Helen had already collected the letters and just needed the flag. Anyway, they gave her the ticket. She screamed 'A flag? I don't believe it,' ran in and got the $100. She said, 'Now we're going to eat steak.' But I said no, we're going to have to pay the gas bill. I don't know if she cried, but I think she did."

The first year the going was hard and there was almost a complete turnover in the NFWA's membership. But gradually the movement began to catch on as Chavez used the tactics he had learned in the CSO. He would send his older children—the Chavezes now have eight—into the fields with leaflets inviting the workers to come to him with their grievances. "If I thought someone had been cheated, I'd raise hell," Chavez says. "You always knew a friendly priest who would pay a call, a friendly lawyer who would write a letter threatening suit." By reading a government manual, he learned how to keep books, and started a credit union for NFWA members. Helen Chavez quit work in the fields and came in to run it.

The eventuality of a major strike was always in the back of Chavez's mind, but he wanted to proceed cautiously. "You can't strike and organize at the same time," he told me. "If you don't have the organization, the strike is going to be broken, don't you worry about that." By 1965, the NFWA had enrolled 1,700 families, and Chavez twice used its strength to force pay raises from growers in the outlying towns around Delano.

"Our first strike was in May of '65, a small one, but it prepared us for the big one," Chavez recalls. "A farm worker from McFarland came to see me. He said he was sick and tired of how people working the roses were being treated, and he was willing to 'go the limit.' The people wanted union recognition, but the real issue, as in most cases when you begin, was wages. They were promised nine dollars a thousand, but they were actually getting $6.50 and seven dollars for grafting roses. Most of them signed cards and gave us the right to bargain for them. We chose the biggest company, with about eighty-five employees, not counting the irrigators and supervisors, and we held a series of meetings to prepare the strike and call the vote. There would be no picket line. Everyone pledged on their honor not to break the strike.

"Early on the first morning of the strike, we sent out ten cars to check the people's homes. We found lights in five or six homes and knocked on the doors. The men were getting up and we'd say, 'Where are you going?' They would dodge, 'Oh, uh . . . I was just getting up, you know.' We'd say, 'Well, you're not going to work, are you?' And they'd say no. Dolores Huerta (a vice president of the NFWA), who was driving the green panel truck, saw a light in one house where four rose workers lived. They told her they were going to work, even after she reminded them of their pledge. So she moved the truck so that it blocked their driveway, turned off the key, put it in her purse and and sat there alone.

"That morning the company foreman was madder than hell and refused to talk to us. None of the grafters had shown up for work. At 10:30 we started to go to the company office, but it occurred to us that maybe a woman would have a better chance. So Dolores knocked on the office door, saying, 'I'm Dolores Huerta from the National Farm Workers' Association.' 'Get out,' the man said, 'you Communist. Get out.' I guess they were expecting us, because as Dolores stood arguing with him, the cops came and told her to leave. She left."

After four days, the company settled with a wage increase and the workers went back on the job. Several months later, the NFWA negotiated another wage increase at a ranch outside Delano. But despite these successes, Chavez still did not feel that the NFWA was sufficiently strong to call a full-scale strike against the massed power of Delano's growers. One afternoon I asked him when he thought the NFWA would have been powerful enough in terms of membership, organization, and strike funds to call the kind of walkout he envisioned. "All things considered," he said, "I think we would have been ready in the fall of 1968."

SEVEN

The strike began three years ahead of schedule. The fuse was lit in the Coachella Valley south of Delano, where, in the spring of 1965, Filipino grape pickers, most of whom were members of the AFL-CIO's Agricultural Workers' Organizing Committee, balked at being paid less than the *braceros* who worked beside them in the fields. Under a U. S. Department of Labor edict, the *braceros* were getting $1.40 an hour base pay, while domestic workers were receiving twenty to thirty cents an hour less, in spite of the Labor Department's stipulation that domestics were in no case to be paid less than the *braceros*. Joined by several hundred Mexican-American pickers, the Filipinos staged a walkout. After ten days, the Coachella Valley growers capitulated and boosted the wage rate for domestics to $1.40 an hour.

The matter might have ended there, had grape growers up through the Valley acknowledged the increase of the Coachella ranchers. But when the Filipinos and Mexican-Americans drifted north to Delano after the end of the Coachella harvest, local growers offered them the same lower pay scales they had struck against in the south. "Naturally they wanted the same pay," I was told one day by Larry Itliong, the chief AWOC organizer in Delano. He is a tough, wiry little Filipino with a crew cut, thick black-rimmed glasses, and three fingers missing on his right hand. "So the workers came to us and asked if we would represent them. They were mainly Filipinos. So we made a representation to the growers by registered mail. Five out of the nine growers we sent letters to accepted them, but none of them showed up at the meeting. This was reported to the workers and right away they wanted to go out on strike. I told them what they were in for. I told them, 'If you go out, you're going to go hungry, lose your car, maybe lose your wife.' They got mad at me for saying that. So I asked who wanted to go out on the picket line. Of the two hundred people at the meeting, only one volunteered. I was disgusted and said, 'Go back to work, don't bother me.'

"Well, they must have thought it over because next day a delegation came to me and said they wanted to strike. I told them, 'Yeah, but you want me to do all the work.' But this time they assured me they would cooperate. All they wanted was one favor. They said if they went out on the picket line they wanted to picket someone else's boss, not their own. They said, 'I work for my boss twenty years. He's a good guy. I picket someone else's boss; someone else picket my boss.' They really identified with their bosses, so I agreed to that. Then I sent a second set of registered letters to the growers giving the time of a meeting at Filipino Hall. Not one showed up. So on the evening of September 7 my people voted to go out. The next morning, at nine camps, the workers solidly refused to go to work. They just stayed in the camps. The bosses figured, 'Let them stay. In five days, these guys will be hungry and begging to go back to work.' Well, they were wrong. On the fifth day, the bosses began to get scab labor. From the Mexicans in Delano, from Arvin, from all over. Our people wanted to beat up the scabs. That's when I went to see Cesar and asked him to help me."

Chavez was in a quandary. Relations between AWOC and the NFWA had never been strong. Chavez had twice refused offers to join AWOC, and at the rank-and-file level, there was an undertow of racial antagonism between the predominantly Filipino AWOC and the predominantly Mexican NFWA. More importantly, Chavez was reluctant to incur the risk of failure by committing his ill-prepared forces to a situation he did not control. "That morning of September 8, a strike was the furthest thing from my mind," he told me. "The first I heard of it was when people came to me and said the Filipinos had gone out. They were mad that the Filipinos weren't working and the Mexicans were. All I could think was, 'Oh God, we're not ready for a strike.' "

Within the NFWA, however, there was a feeling that if Chavez did not call a strike now, ready or not, he would be forever loath to take the chance. Backed into a corner, his hand forced, Chavez finally decided that it would be far worse to ignore the strike than to join it. On the night of September 16, he called for a strike vote. Hundreds of workers were packed into the Filipino Hall on the West Side of Delano. Chavez stood before the crowd, dressed in work pants and an old sport shirt. "You are here to discuss a matter which is of extreme importance to yourselves, your families, and your community," he said. "So let's get to the subject at hand. A hundred and fifty-five years ago, in the state of Guanajoto in Mexico, a padre proclaimed the struggle for liberty. He was killed, but ten years later Mexico won its independence. We Mexicans here in the United States, as well as all other farm workers, are engaged in another struggle for the freedom and dignity which poverty denies us. But it must not be a violent struggle, even if violence is used against us. Violence can only hurt us and our cause. The law is for us as well as the ranchers. The strike was begun by the Filipinos, but it is not exclusively for them. Tonight we must decide if we are to join our fellow workers."

The vote for the strike was unanimous. The following Monday, September 20, twelve days after the Filipinos had first refused to work, and with less than $100 in its strike treasury, the NFWA joined AWOC on the picket line, and strike leadership, because of the preponderance of Mexicans involved, passed unofficially but decisively into Chavez's hands. "I'll never forget that first morning," Wendy Goepel, one of the first volunteers to arrive in Delano, told me. "We all got to the office at 3:30 a.m. and just waited for people to show up. We were all very nervous. We didn't know if they would. It was like that moment at the beginning of a party when the host and hostess wonder if anyone will come, if they got the date right, or if the invitations were sent out. But then they began to filter in, and Cesar went around telling them if they had a gun or a knife or anything sharp to leave it behind."

The character of the strike was molded immediately. Chavez knew that without outside help the strike would be broken, as had every farm labor dispute in the past. He also knew that the only way to get that help was to spotlight the situation in Delano as a moral issue. But the old-line Anglo labor organizers within AWOC vigorously resisted Chavez's plan to call on the clergy and civil-rights groups for support. This was particularly true of Al Green, the head of AWOC, a man characterized by another Cali-

fornia labor leader as a "heavy-handed gringo." "Green
didn't even want me to *talk* to Cesar," Larry Itliong told
me. "He wrote me a letter that said not to have a goddam
thing to do with the NFWA." I asked Chavez the reasons
for this opposition. "They just couldn't make us out," he
said. "The NFWA didn't speak the proper language, you
know, worker solidarity, the union above all. They
thought it was treason to ask for outside help, because it
implied that the union wasn't capable of doing things on
its own." To a certain extent, this sentiment still prevailed
when I arrived in Delano the following July. One day I
walked into a grower's office shortly after an old-time
AWOC organizer had left. "You know what he told me?"
the grower asked. "He said that if we had joined AWOC at
the start, they would have taken care of that son of a bitch
Chavez for us."

From the outset Chavez counted on the support of the
Church. It was a foregone conclusion that he would be
aided by the California Migrant Ministry, an adjunct of
the Division of Home Missions of the National Council of
Churches. The California Migrant Ministry had for years
been intimately connected with farm labor problems. But
Chavez was also convinced that he would get other, less
institutional clerical support. "This didn't start when the
strike began," he told me one day. "I've been making
friends with the clergy for sixteen years, ever since I was
with the CSO. How could the Catholic clergy stay out of
this one? All the Mexicans are Catholic. And the Church is
the one group that isn't expecting anything from us.
They're not doing any politicking among us. All the other
groups, the unions, the civil-rights groups, they all want
something in return for their support. Not the Church. I

would have been surprised if I hadn't gotten their support after all these years."

Clerical support, however, drove a wedge down the Valley. In Delano, the local Catholic clergy was on the spot. Most of the financial support for the Church came from the Anglos, while the Mexicans made up the bulk of the parishioners. So the priests of Delano chose to sit squarely, if uncomfortably, on the fence. "If the growers have a poor year, the Church feels the effect of a poor harvest," said Father James Dillon, pastor of St. Mary's Catholic Church in Delano. "We took the stand that it's not our place to take sides. It would be just as wrong to be on the growers' side as it would to be on the side of the workers. The rightness or the wrongness of the strike is something I can't answer. I think it's an economic issue. It's not a moral issue." Other Valley priests openly declared their opposition to any state or federal legislation giving farm workers the right to organize. "They have the right," declared Monsignor Daniel J. Keenan of Huron. "God Almighty gave them that." He left the impression that it was blasphemous to suggest that the Almighty needed Washington in his corner.

Other churchmen lent their support to Chavez in direct defiance of their clerical superiors. Though ordered to avoid public involvement in the dispute, Father James L. Vizzard of the National Catholic Rural Life Conference nevertheless came to Delano and charged that California's Catholic leaders were not only "frozen with fear" but had also "abandoned their sheep when they were under attack." Father Vizzard's statement stirred the wrath of Bishop A. J. Willinger, whose Monterey-Fresno diocese included Delano. "There is an old saying, 'If you don't blow your own horn, who is there to blow it for you?' " Bishop Willinger wrote in his diocesan newspaper. "One of the horn blowers of the day is the Reverend James L. Vizzard, S.J. His participation in the dispute at Delano was an act of unadulterated disobedience, insubordination and a breach of office."

California's other six bishops were more judicious. So many priests had pledged to help Chavez that if restrictions were placed on their involvement the Church would find itself in an untenable position. No one saw the situation more clearly than Bishop Hugh Donohoe of Stockton, a slight, white-haired Irishman with a hint of a brogue. "The thinking about our agricultural workers now is to keep them in the poorest part of town and then to get rid of them as quickly as possible after the harvest," he told a California state senate committee investigating the Delano dispute. "The farmer will go broke if he does everything we think should be done. We know that. So the tendency of the farmer is to do nothing, or the very minimum. That can't work either." Under his gentle prodding, California's seven bishops, including Bishop Willinger, on March 16, 1966, released a statement laying down the Church's position on farm labor. It was not a document designed to endear the bishops to the growers, since it called for legislation to bring farm workers under the jurisdiction of the National Labor Relations Act. "This one act will not solve the farm labor problem," the statement said, "but it would be a first and giant step toward a solution. It is becoming evident that unless farm workers are given the chance to organize, they are going to become wards of the state."

With the clergy firmly in his corner, Chavez maneu-

vered his meager forces like a field marshal. He purposely
did not picket certain growers, preferring to keep them for
what he called his "safety valve." There was often work
available at these ranches, and on those days, Chavez
would pull pickets from the line and get them to sign on
with the unstruck growers in order to earn a few days'
wages. Every move of the growers Chavez was quick to
exploit, even when they raised the pickers' base pay from
$1.20 to $1.40 an hour shortly after the strike started.
"Alinsky says you only win your fight through the mis-
takes of the opposition," Chavez told me one day in the
back booth of a West Side coffee shop. "And every time
we moved, they made a mistake immediately. It was a
mistake for them to have a wage increase so soon after the
strike started. We could exploit that. It showed the workers we were being effective. They should have held out,
pretending we were nothing, impressing their crews with
how strong they were. And it was a mistake for them to
move their crews away from the road to the middle of the
field. That showed the crew we were powerful and that
their boss was afraid of us. We could exploit that, too."

By the time I arrived in Delano, ten months after the
strike started, picketing had settled down to both a science
and a routine. This I discovered shortly after dawn one
morning when I joined the picket caravan as it was assem-
bling. There must have been fifteen cars in the caravan,
old two-tone models mostly, of a late-fifties vintage, with
threadbare tires, pitted windshields, and engines that
sounded like broken-down espresso machines. For nearly
half an hour, the caravan drove slowly up and down the
back county roads, looking for crews. From the start, we
were tailed by a Kern County sheriff's car, and when we

crossed County Line Road we were picked up in turn by two Tulare County police cruisers.

The first stop was the farm of a rancher named A. Caratan, where a few workers were desultorily hoeing weeds. Piling out of their cars, the picketers—there were approximately seventy-five—lined up the length of the vineyard and began shouting: "*Viva la huelga.*" Most of the picketers were old men in dilapidated straw hats; the picket captains were younger and there were a few teenagers, including an attractive young girl in a white shirt and pigtails. As I stood in the center of the road watching them, one of the Tulare County sheriff's men pulled up alongside me and asked what I was doing there. He was smoking a cigar and wearing sunglasses and a sky-blue hard plastic hat. The plastic nameplate attached to his gabardine tunic identified him as Sergeant Webb, J.O. At that moment, a grower whom I knew drove up and identified me; on the back seat of the grower's car was a riot gun.

"Christ, I don't know if you're *huelga* people or employers or what," Sergeant Webb apologized. "We've had so goddamn many people out here saying they're reporters, we got to be careful." He perused me carefully. "I see you got a sunburn last Monday," he said pleasantly.

I did not remember seeing Sergeant Webb before.

"At DiGiorgio last week, when they laid off those 190 workers," he said. "I saw you out there. And that little lady with you in the red dress—was that your wife? I thought she was going to melt in the heat."

If ever I had doubts about the card file of 5,000 strike supporters maintained by the sheriff's office, they were dispelled by this exchange. As if to underline it, the other deputy, a huge Negro named E. W. Washington, sidled up to the photographer with me and said, *sotto voce,* "You see that guy with the beard and the camera?" He was referring to the NFWA's official photographer, a young volunteer studying for his M.A. at San Francisco State College. "How about getting a picture of him for me? Every time I try, he turns his head."

The sun glinting off his blue helmet, Sergeant Webb reached into his cruiser, pulled out a bunch of grapes, and offered me some. "God, this is boring," he said. "Nothing much happens any more, and after eight hours we get hot and tired, too. And sure as hell, just when we get hot and a little lax, that's when something will happen. It's not as if this has been going on only a month or so. It's been going on for a long time and a lot of hatred has built up."

Moments later, a picket threw a wadded NFWA authorization slip at one of the field workers. Like a cat, Sergeant Webb bounded across the road to the head picket captain, a handsome youth in his early twenties named Pete Cardenas.

"You can't do that, Pete," he said. (After so many months on picket duty, Webb calls all the picket captains by their first names.) "Sure, I know it's only a piece of paper, but all the foreman knows is he saw somebody throw something. He thinks it's a rock, he might throw a rock back. So don't have your people throw anything, Pete, not even paper. It's going to be a long, hot day out here."

There did not seem to be enough workers in this field to bother with, so the caravan moved on again. "We just birddog them all day long," Sergeant Webb told me. "That's what we call close surveillance." No sooner had the pickets stopped at the next ranch than the foreman pulled his crew into the center of the field. The caravan started again. The sun was high in the sky now and the heat bored down and the cars drove up and down the county roads as if they were not quite sure where they were going. Finally they pulled to a stop at a ranch called Buckman Farms. There were boxes and a portable packing rig by the side of the road, and a radio played Mexican music.

The Brockman vineyard had been leased by a grower called Missakian, a large, formidable-looking man with a slight mustache, and thinning hair plastered across his skull. He drove up and posted himself by a packing truck just inside the property line, staring impassively at the pickets. With a bullhorn, one of the picketers called for unity among the farm workers and told the pickers that their wages had been raised the previous fall only through union pressure. "Do you want your children to be field workers, too, or do they deserve a chance?" he shouted. "Does your miserable boss give you job security?"

Missakian moved away from his truck wearily. "You start talking about their miserable boss, you come over here and talk to me," he said, beckoning for the picket to cross the property line. "You hear," he said, his voice rising slightly. "You talk to me."

"The miserable bosses try to call us Communists," the picket with the bullhorn said in English. "But your boss's son, he went to school while the Mexican-Americans went off to war and were killed for their country. We died for our country in Europe, in Korea, and they try to call us Communists. Your boss's son, he was deferred. Were you?"

The crew went about their work as if they did not hear. It seemed a play in which everyone knew his role. On the front lawn of the house across from the vineyard, a group of adults watched the display, shucking peas and drinking lemonade. The pigtailed teenager on the picket line was carrying a *huelga* flag, and I saw her smile and wave surreptitiously with one finger to an equally young picker, who just as slyly smiled back.

"They don't spout so much of that Communist propaganda as they used to," Deputy Washington said, offering me a glass of water from the canteen in the front seat of his car. "That used to make me mad. They don't like America, why don't they leave it? And *filthy*. That Berkeley bunch, that SNCC crowd, they were the filthiest crowd I ever did see. I said to one of them, I said, 'Don't you ever take a bath?' And he said to me, 'What's it to you?' And I told him, 'You just show up here tomorrow without taking a bath and I'll show you what it is to me.' And he said, 'You can't pull me in for that.' And I said to him, 'You just try me.'"

He took another swig of water and pointed at the pickets. "Look at those people," he said. "They aren't workers, most of them. A lot of them's on welfare. The county's paying them and they're out here trying to start a fight. I always said, we ain't never had a war in this country, and these people are trying to start one." I refrained from mentioning the Civil War, for Deputy Washington had taken another tack. "A man sweats blood trying to make something, he's got a right to try and save it," he said. "These people are trying to take it away from him."

EIGHT

Just how many workers Chavez's picket tactics pulled out of the fields at the beginning of the strike is a point that will probably remain forever moot. "I would say there's been a steady concealment on both sides of this dispute about what the facts are," Harlan Hagen, the grower-oriented former congressman whose district encompassed Delano and who was defeated in the 1966 election by Republican Bob Mathias, the former Olympic decathlon champion, told the U. S. Senate Subcommittee on Migratory Labor in a hearing at Visalia in March, 1966. "I don't think the union wants to disclose what their membership is and I don't think the growers want to disclose how many people left work and how many people they brought in from the outside. You get two stories. And I don't see how you might verify them." The most grandiose NFWA claim is that 5,000 workers walked out, while the most that the growers will admit to is several hundred. Part of the difficulty in getting an accurate count is that when workers walked off their jobs in sympathy with the NFWA, they would almost immediately leave Delano to look for work elsewhere. This proved to be a particular hardship for the NFWA when California Department of Employment officials arrived in Delano to certify the strikes against each individual grower. In only fifteen of the thirty-one cases investigated, did they find that workers actually left their jobs because of the dispute. Often the NFWA was hard put to get three workers from an individual ranch to remain in town for the Employment Department's interview.

Today Delano growers point to the scarcity of certified depositions as proof that Chavez's strike was a failure. "The workers voted every day of the harvest," Martin Zaninovich, one of the bigger Delano growers, told the senate subcommittee. "How? The size of our crop and the efficiency with which it was harvested are votes that even the most prejudiced person cannot ignore or submerge with half truths or false or misleading statements. They have voted with their feet, so to speak, by going to work regularly in our vineyards. The proof is that some 5,000 of our regular workers stayed on the job and picked the largest crop of grapes in history."

Zaninovich was challenged by Senator Robert Kennedy. "I don't think it answers the question for you to come in here and say to this subcommittee, 'None of these people want to join the unions. I can tell you they don't want to join the unions.' I mean, I've heard people say quite frankly down in Mississippi, 'You don't understand. Negroes don't want to vote.'" Kennedy elaborated on this statement later in the hearing. "If the people don't want a union or want a particular union, let them decide," he said. "I don't think you can say, 'Because our grapes were picked last year, therefore nobody wants a union.' There were an awful lot of people who worked during the 1920's to 1930's who were working, who were staying on the job not because they didn't want a union but because they had no financial means of surviving. And when you're talking about having meals to feed your children and money to buy clothes and to continue an education, then you'll have to make the judgment of whether you're going to be able to go out on strike or whether you're going to have to go to work."

There was one opportunity to settle the conflicting claims about the number of strikers, but the growers let it slip by when, almost to a man, they refused to let the Employment Department check their payroll records to see how many workers had left their employ after September 20. This was a major tactical blunder which lent credence to the NFWA claim that the ranchers were afraid to open up their payrolls since that would show beyond doubt how many workers had struck. One day I asked Bruno Dispoto, perhaps the Delano grower most violently and vituperatively opposed to Chavez, why he had refused to show his payroll records to the Labor Department people. "For one simple reason," he said. "I had no problem. I lost only one man." I remarked that he then had nothing to lose by opening his records, and everything to gain, since the records could prove conclusively that the NFWA's claims were patently untrue. "We have a tremendous turnover here," he replied easily. "Even if a worker walked out for another reason, woman trouble, say, they'd interpret it as a strike walkout." Since the state still had to obtain an affidavit from the worker stating that the strike was the reason for his departure, this did not seem a valid rationale, but it was one I heard repeatedly from local growers.

To undercut the NFWA, the ranchers announced their preference for another union, the Kern-Tulare Independent Farm Workers, which blossomed into existence after the strike began. It was not that the growers had changed their basic ideas about a farm union. But two of the five directors of the Kern-Tulare Farm Workers Union were labor contractors who supplied pickers to the local growers. Throughout the Valley, contractors regarded Chavez as the antichrist, because one of his stated aims was to do away with the whole labor contracting setup. Hoping to capitalize on this anti-Chavez sentiment, the growers bestowed their blessing on the Kern-Tulare Farm Workers; the contractors, after all, were a known quantity, and not likely to rock the boat. But a contractor is an employer, and under California law, any association financed or directed even in part by an employer cannot be construed as a labor organization. Thus the Kern-Tulare Independent Farm Workers came to an early end.

The growers, however, had other cards to play. To replace the struck workers, they began in the fall of 1965 to import pickers from the California and Texas border towns. The growers claim that only seventy-seven such strikebreakers were brought into Delano, a figure challenged by signed depositions in the NFWA files, making it just one more case of Delano mathematics. One El Paso, Texas, contractor has admitted that he recruited 200 workers for the Delano vineyards. Two who made the trip from El Paso were Olivas Martinez and Armando Alvarez Lopez, both of whom are "green card" holders (Mexican nationals with United States work permits) from across the border in Juarez. Under federal law, green-card workers are supposed to be told when a strike is in progress, but this detail was omitted by the Texas labor contractor who recruited them for the Delano fields. With thirty-eight other workers, Martinez and Lopez were bused from Texas to Delano, where they began to work for the

DiGiorgio Corporation, the largest rancher in the area. They were paid $1.40 an hour or $12.60 a day, from which $2.25 a day was deducted for room and board at the labor camp where they were put up. Every day for lunch they were served boiled potatoes and white beans. At breakfast, the first workers in received three eggs, the rest two; there weren't enough eggs to go around, the cook told them, because the chickens were on strike. The first payroll week, the two men earned $68 each, $35 of which was deducted for board and their bus fare from Texas; the remaining $33 they sent back to their wives. Though the labor contractor in Texas had guaranteed that they would have eight or nine hours of work seven days a week, they were given only three days' work on their second week in Delano, and each grossed $37.80. From this, $32.80 was deducted for meals and the balance of their bus fare, leaving each with a net of five dollars for the week's work.

Under these circumstances, many of the strikebreakers quit and joined the NFWA, thereby compounding Chavez's worst problem—lack of money. From the outset, the cost of the strike had been prohibitive. By the summer of 1966, it was costing the NFWA $25,000 a month just to keep its head above water. Gasoline alone cost $4,000 a month; the telephone, another $1,600. In addition, the NFWA absorbed all the expenses, including rent, food, and car payments, of the hundred families on permanent picket duty. Chavez's money problems were perversely complicated shortly after the strike started, when Sargent Shriver's Office of Economic Opportunity gave the NFWA $265,000 to begin a community organization project. Though the OEO demanded that the strike and the community project be kept separate, the grant not unexpect edly ran into a hurricane of opposition from growers, who saw it as a federal subsidy to keep the strike going. Nor was Chavez himself too happy with the outlay. He knew it would be next to impossible to keep the strike and the organizing project from overlapping. Furthermore, he did not have enough trained organizers available to direct both. Finally he asked the OEO to keep the funds in escrow until the strike was over, and Shriver, under pressure from both growers and the town of Delano, was only too happy to do so.

The bills, however, still had to be paid, and the money came in from everywhere in every way. The largest contributor was Walter Reuther's United Auto Workers, who earmarked $5,000 a month to Delano, split evenly between AWOC, which was an AFL-CIO affiliate, and the NFWA, which was not. Other unions held gate collections and sent the proceeds to Delano. (Harry Bridges's ILWU was even more strategically helpful. On the San Francisco docks, Bridges's longshoremen refused to load Delano grapes on the Orient-bound *President Wilson*.) Folksinger Pete Seeger gave a concert for the NFWA in Los Angeles and turned the receipts over to the strike fund. But most of the money in those early months came in coins and small bills, the average contribution being $5.56. Dances were held where guests paid for their tickets with cans of food for the strikers, the fourth grade at the Holy Angels School in Sacramento held a cupcake sale, collecting five dollars for the NFWA, and a one-legged ex-farm worker contributed his entire disability check. The first Christmas of the strike, unions and private donors sent to Delano 400 turkeys, 1,000 pounds of rice, and 1,000 Christmas stockings packed with basketballs, footballs, dolls, and other toys. A strike toy store was set up, and farm worker parents, based on their service to the strike, received toy coupons which enabled them to select gifts for their children. The entire Christmas operation was called by one Delano grower a "stunt," a remark that brought even more food and gifts to the strikers.

Each $5.56 meant a great deal to the strikers, a fact I did not fully appreciate until I saw the camp the NFWA maintains across from the county dump on the western edge of Delano. At one time a labor camp, it is run by Julio Hernandez, a beefy, phlegmatic officer of the NFWA, and consists of a Nissen hut where food and provisions are stored, a ramshackle mess hall, a roofed but open-sided auto-body shop, at one end of which is a tumbledown grandstand where the strikers sometimes gather for meetings, and a brand-new air-conditioned trailer from which the NFWA's resident nurse and volunteer doctors dispense medical care to the strikers and their families. Surrounding the camp is a weathered, sagging fence on which are whitewashed two slogans: VIVA PANCHO VILLA and JUAREZ, ZAPATA, CHAVEZ.

The most striking fact of the camp is the contrast between the high spirits of the strikers and the conditions of their existence. On my first visit, I ran into two young picket captains Indian-wrestling outside the mess hall. One wore a button that said: "I'm an alcoholic—in case of emergency, give me a beer." The interior of the mess hall looks like a hash house on some sweltering, God-forsaken back road. The blower that day was out of order, a regular occurrence, and the heat was almost viscous, yet none of the picketers or volunteers shoveling in eggs and beans at the stools around the counter seemed in the least uncomfortable.

From week to week, Hernandez never knows if he will have enough food to feed the strikers and their families. Each week the strikers need 200 pounds of tortilla flour, 100 pounds of dry red beans, 100 pounds of pinto beans, 200 pounds of sugar, 200 pounds of potatoes, 50 pounds of coffee, 50 cases of canned fruits and vegetables, and enough powdered or canned milk for 450 children. Every scrap of food is donated by friends of the strike all over California, and hardly a day goes by when a station wagon or pickup truck does not arrive with new provisions. ("Some people even donate cars," Hernandez told me. "Not their number-one car, maybe; their number-six or number-seven car, by the looks of them when we get them.") One union has pledged a hundred dozen eggs a week (in all, the strikers use 200 dozen); another, forty pounds of hamburger; and a bakery in Los Angeles sends up, daily, a hundred loaves of day-old bread. (The NFWA asked a bakery in Delano for its day-old bread and was flatly turned down. No food at all, in fact, has been donated by townspeople.) Every afternoon, a delegated number of strikers' wives lined up outside the storehouse for their week's provisions. One day I drove out to the camp and was told that supplies were so low that no food was being passed out. An emergency call had gone out for food, but in the meantime all the strikers and their families had to eat in the mess hall, where usually only the volunteers, pickets, and bachelor strikers ate. It was three days before stocks were replenished and normal distribution could begin again.

Under such a haphazard system, the strikers' diet could scarcely be called balanced. Except for the eggs, they have had little fresh food since the strike began. Everything is canned or dried, even the milk. One day in the storehouse I saw case upon case of canned pork and beans (topped by the curious contribution of one donor—a bottle of Angostura bitters). "We can never be sure what we're going to get," Hernandez's wife told me. "I guess pork and beans are the cheapest thing to buy. It's not part of the Mexican diet, but if it comes to starvation, I guess we'll eat it."

I was particularly interested in how the strikers had fared under this regimen, and on another afternoon I talked to Peggy McGivern, the NFWA's resident nurse. She is a tall, attractive, almost catatonically quiet young woman who had nursed at the Stanford University Medical Center. She had originally arrived in Delano for only a short period, but when the pressing need for daily medical care became apparent, she stayed on. Most of the equipment in the trailer, which is rented from a firm in San Jose, has been donated through the American Friends' Service Committee; the drugs are mainly pharmaceutical company samples given by doctors throughout the state. No Delano doctor has ever offered to help at the clinic. Miss McGivern said that the NFWA had only approached one, whose nurse announced that the doctor was not taking any new patients; after that, no other local physician was approached. Instead, volunteer doctors, usually from Los Angeles and San Francisco, came to Delano twice a week on an irregular rotating basis.

The fact that there were so few serious health problems amazed one volunteer doctor, Jerome Lackner, a Fresno physician who spent the first Christmas of the strike working at the NFWA clinic in Delano. "I was asked by the nurse to make a house call on a person who was unable to come to the clinic," he said. "The husband, who had just two days previously joined the strike, came to the clinic and asked us to see his wife. We followed him to a very nice, relatively newly built bungalow apartment. Not bad-looking, I thought. It had a bedroom, a small living room, and a little kitchen. It would have been an ideal residence for a young couple without children. Inside were a mother and seven children. The stench of putrefying, necrotic tissue filled the interior of the house. A baby of eighteen months lay asleep on the bare floor in front of a blazing gas heater. The mother lay sick on the couch. She had delivered her seventh baby at home, with the aid of a neighbor lady, several days before I arrived. There was a considerable loss of blood. She was pale and febrile, appeared very toxic and had a profuse malodorous lochia, which she absorbed on towels stuffed into her underwear. It was Christmas Eve. I wondered who would take care of the children when she died. The new baby was asleep in the crib.

"I called the county hospital and talked to the admitting resident. Prompt evaluation and probable admission was concurred on. I phoned the emergency room four times in the next five to six hours before the poor man showed up with his wife. Even then, it was hard for me to understand how it could take anyone so long. The next day he explained he had gone to the NFWA office to get money for gasoline. He had to find a friend whose car would make the trip. He had to place the six older children with a friend who had seven children. Once in Bakersfield, he had to find the house of a relative with enough know-how to bottle-feed and care for the new baby, and then the relative pointed him in the direction of the hospital, which he had trouble finding at twelve midnight, as he had never been there before. Fortunately the patient responded well to what must have been technically excellent treatment and was later discharged to return to her family.

"Another time nurse and I called to see a sick baby and I asked the parents to turn on the light in the bedroom so I might see the ailing tyke, only to find that the only functioning light bulb in the entire house was hung from a wire in the kitchen. I was embarrassed by my *faux pas* and wondered if they were disturbed by my matter-of-factly affluent assumption that every room would have a light bulb. One other experience, regarding my one journey while in Kern County to the elegant side of the tracks. At my insistence, the nurse and I spent the better part of an hour in dialogue with a lay official of the Kern County Medical Society. I wanted first merely to inform him of my presence and ask him if there was any advice he could give me. Yes, he had lots of advice to give me: Be sure my malpractice insurance covers me outside my own county; go home and care for the people in my county; farm workers are overpaid and could well afford the modest fees of local doctors if only they would work harder and be more frugal. All this he told me as an objective citizen, a neutral observer in the struggle in which I was a biased participant. I was overwhelmed by his assistance, his neutrality, but mostly by his authoritative understanding of prevailing farm wages. I was reassured about all, however, when he explained that his information was firsthand, since he had business holdings in several large grape ranches."

NINE

The rights and interests of the laboring man will be protected and taken care of, not by the labor agitators, but by the Christian men to whom God in His infinite wisdom has given control of the property interests of this country.

George Baer, President, Reading Coal & Iron Co., 1900

These pickers don't want a union. They've got a real fine relationship with the employers. Really personal. A union would destroy it.

Joseph Brosmer, Agricultural Labor Bureau, 1966

On the grape ranches, there had developed an almost psychotic aversion to Chavez. Almost to the saturation point, growers had absorbed the propaganda of their own lobby, which for generations has boosted the notion that agriculture is entitled to special immunities from the effects of bad weather, competition, and even labor problems. Unfailingly, the farm lobby points out that in 1935 Congress specifically exempted agricultural workers from coverage under Senator Robert Wagner's National Labor Relations Act. The ostensible reason was that farm workers are not engaged in interstate commerce, but the actual power of farm state solons stymied any real discussion of the problem. Ever since, the farm lobby has used this benchmark exemption to frustrate any minimum-wage or collective bargaining legislation designed to benefit farm workers. The campaign has gone to such absurd lengths that only last year the farm lobby railed righteously against proposed child-labor laws. "We believe that the prohibition against employment of migratory minors twelve or thirteen years of age is a prohibition that would do more harm than good," a spokesman for the American Farm Bureau told a United States Senate subcommittee. "We do not share the view that employment of young people is 'exploitation' of their labor. Exposure to work at a comparatively early age is an important part of the educational process and the development of maturity."

Beneath the farm lobby's cant, there are more viable arguments against allowing agricultural workers to organize. The growers' strongest point is that a harvest strike could cause a whole year's crop to rot in the fields. It was the rare grower who did not tell me that agriculture is not like industry, that an assembly line could increase production at the end of a strike, while a farmer either had to wait until the next year to recoup his losses or faced bankruptcy. But organized labor counters with the argument that harvest strikes occur only when ranchers refuse to recognize a union. They maintain that if a union were recognized, a contract could be written that would preclude the possibility of a harvest strike. "The grower naturally fears that he will be struck just at the time his crop is ready for harvest," says Thomas L. Harris of the Teamsters Union. "As long as the grower has no collective bargaining agreement, we would hope that the threat would remain. But this threat is one that a grower who genuinely engages in collective bargaining can very greatly reduce, if not entirely eliminate. After all, most canneries, like most farmers, are particularly vulnerable to a strike at the height of a season. This problem was recognized many years ago. Consequently, most of our Teamster cannery contracts expire on February 28, when cannery processing is at a minimum. Or, in other words, when the immediate economic power of our cannery unions is at a minimum. Negotiations for a new contract habitually extend over the next month or so, and it is quite customary for our members to work on a day-to-day basis, without a contract, pending conclusion of negotiations. Since 1937, there have been only three significant strikes in the cannery industry. The last strike occurred in 1956 for pension benefits and lasted approximately ten days."

On this point at least, there is room for argument and compromise. But in Delano, growers took their stand on the century-old line that their workers are perfectly happy and don't want a union. "What is the problem?" Bruno Dispoto asked me one day. "The workers have always gotten along well with us. They make good money. Some have beautiful homes. They own cars. They are our neighbors here and we were getting along well until the troublemakers started." To back up this claim, the growers point out that the 1965 grape crop was the largest in California history. So many grapes were picked, in fact, that the price of wine grapes fell from $57 a ton to $20 and under. "We would have been better off if the strike had been halfway effective," says Bruce Obbink, a representative of the California Council of Growers. "If they left half the harvest unpicked, the higher price would have held and the growers could have made some money."

Among the growers, the feeling persists that the pickers are the last of the free spirits, holding all the cards in their hands. "Those clouds start bumping around in the sky and the workers begin taking off," Bruno Dispoto told me in his office one afternoon. "See, they can bargain, because if they do take off, we're in trouble. They don't have a union card, but they're in a top bargaining position. Some want to work for two weeks, others for two months. That's the way these people operate. If my workers were unionized, they'd have shackles around their necks. Can they work one day and take off two if they feel like it then? No, of course not. They wouldn't have the freedom our workers have now. This working one day and taking off two, that's the nature of these people."

The most cogent objection to this sentiment was raised not by the NFWA but by the attorney of one of the largest growers in Delano when I talked to him one afternoon in San Francisco. "The growers have put on a miserable performance," he said. "They had a case and they didn't present it. They were sullen and stolid and the only thing they could think of was calling everyone a Communist. They're so paternalistic. They don't understand why people want to be responsible for their own condition. All this stuff they give about 'We know our men and they're happy.' It doesn't ring true and they know it doesn't ring true. Look, the picker is the lowest man on the economic totem pole. It doesn't matter how much you pay him an hour. People live by the year, not by the hour. That's what the growers refuse to understand. The pickers are just miserable sons of bitches who have no control over their lives. Most of them don't speak any English and haven't known anything better, so the growers have been able to get away with this paternalism. They'll show you their books until the sun goes down and tell you they'll never make a profit with a union. And the conditions have always been right for them to think this way. You can't really blame them for not wanting someone to come in and tell them the way to run their business. But they'll tell you they can't put toilets in the fields because it costs too much money. They'll bring out their books and show how a field toilet is the difference between breaking even and going broke. But the history of the labor movement shows that management doesn't go broke by recognizing a union. That's what Chavez has going for him—seventy-five years of labor history. But you listen to the growers and you'd think that the labor movement is just some kind of passing fancy."

Yet there was something about the growers that made me indescribably sad, for, as a generation of Southern novelists recognized, the drama lies not in the gain but in the loss. What Chavez was challenging was a way of life that, to the growers, and indeed to much of California, seemed as God-given and endemic to the Valley as the summer sun and the winter floods. A heady history of casually breaking farm labor strikes had given the growers an emotional investment in not yielding to this one. For a grower to do so, no matter how, privately, he thought it might be the right thing, would have been a breach of community faith, an act that would forever tarnish his credentials among his neighbors. This was made abundantly clear when I was told of the gentle complaint made by the wife of the manager of the Schenley ranch, which just before Easter, 1966, became the first in Delano to capitulate to Chavez. Afterwards, she said, she was snubbed in the beauty parlor by the wives of other ranchers, was not invited to several large parties, and she and her husband were "avoided" by other growers in the Elks club.

What made the growers even more embattled was the feeling that they had been abandoned by the very interests to whom they had looked for support. Neither industry nor the banks rallied to their defense. The reasons are easy to tabulate. In the first place, the huge federal subsidies to farmers have always been resented by other businessmen. Even more important, industry has dealt with organized labor for decades and found it, at worst, a tenable inconvenience. "Unions are something you have to deal with," an officer at one of California's largest banks told me. "They're irritating at times, but they're not ogres. So why should the growers get upset. They've had a free ride without unions for a longer time than industry ever did."

Perhaps I have already suggested that these are not the growers of the liberal imagination, the hard-drinking, fast-wheeling planters with white hats and bullwhips and frivolous wives, arrogant heirs to absentee fortunes. Only two of the thirty-eight growers in Delano are absentee landlords (although those two, DiGiorgio and Schenley, are the two biggest). The rest are for the most part those second-generation Americans of Yugoslavian descent, men whose immigrant fathers came in the 1920's to a land still little more than a desert, trying to cash in on the American dream. But they had arrived a century too late. The frontier was ended; to the west lay the Pacific Ocean and around them lapped the twentieth century and the complexities of industrial society. They are clannish and stubborn, and because they arrived so late, they cling tighter to the frontier mentality than do the men whose great-grandfathers helped to create it. They still speak in the accents of their fathers and not in the featureless inflections of affluent California, and they cannot believe that they might be in the wrong. They think they are fighting Cesar Chavez, but they are fighting time and they do not know it—and there is no more ruthless or relentless an enemy.

Of all the growers in Delano, the one least leery of outsiders is a stocky, middle-aged man named Jack Pandol. Pandol talks incessantly with a kind of exasperated good humor, punctuating his remarks with emphatic finger-shaking and fist-slamming. When he stops to chat with his workers, he lapses into pidgin Spanish delivered with a Yugoslavian accent. ("That's the vernacular deal when we talk to our employees," he explains.) I talked with him half a dozen times in the weeks I was in Delano; he was never less than open and seemed truly bewildered by the demands of the NFWA. "What's Chavez's program?" he asked me the first time I met him. "Give us a program and we'll try to find some meeting ground. We're not inhuman. But all Chavez is trying to do is replace my power structure with his." There, in a nutshell, is the problem of Delano.

Work is the entire life of the Delano growers. "Around here, all we ever talk about is grapes," Pandol told me. "My brother-in-law is in cotton and alfalfa and we don't have much in common. He talks about alfalfa and I talk about grapes." The Slavs tend to stick together and have little social intercourse with the non-Slav growers. Nor do they wander far from their vineyards; there is neither a Slav lawyer nor a Slav doctor in Delano. Largely because of the language difficulty, the first generation of Slav growers married other Slavs, and this tendency still prevails; Pandol and one of his brothers, for example, both married Zaninoviches. Two or three times a year, there are dances in the Slav Hall, and on the second and fourth Wednesday every month there is a growers' luncheon. Only Slavs and people married to Slavs can be members of the Slav Club. It is too hot to play golf on the new nine-hole course in Delano, and entertainment generally means a night out for dinner in Bakersfield. And until the strike brought them together, however tentatively, there was a chasm between the townspeople and the growers. "Maybe they thought the growers made too much money," Pandol's wife, a handsome, gray-haired woman, told me. "The town didn't like to admit how tied they are to the farmers, how dependent they are on us."

A frequent theme in Pandol's conversation, and indeed in that of all the Delano growers, is the low return on investment characteristic of American agriculture. With his two brothers, Pandol runs a 2,000-acre ranch, which with all its equipment and improvements—trucks, tractors, fork lifts, sheds, box-making machinery, and refrigerating systems—is worth in the vicinity of $4,000,000. In the five years between 1961 and 1965, Pandol told me, bringing out his income-tax statements for verification, the sales of his Three Brothers ranch averaged $1,350,000 a year. Over the same five-year period, the average annual profit was $22,500. "A business that grosses that much and nets that little is in trouble," Pandol said. "That's $7,500 a year for each of my brothers and me. I could go out as a grape salesman and make a hell of a lot more than that."

Early one morning, Pandol picked me up and drove me

out to a field where he had a crew girdling vines. By the side of the vineyard there was a dusty pickup with a bumper sticker that said, "I Fight Poverty—I Work." We watched the crew for a few minutes and then he brought one of the workers over.

"How many kids you got?" Pandol asked.

"Two married," the worker replied.

"That's not how it's done," Pandol laughed. "You got to get your kids to go out and work for you and you go on relief. That's how it's done these days."

Nodding and smiling agreeably, the picker walked back into the field. Pandol than hailed a crew foreman standing by the side of his pickup. "Hey, Ted," he said, "tell us how Chavez is nonviolent."

The foreman was a small neat man named Ted Ramos who spoke in thickly accented English. "They used to shout at me, 'Hey, Ted, your name's on our list. Aren't you afraid?' No, I wasn't afraid. Chavez's people, they'd scratch the workers' cars with nails, and then lodge nails under the wheels of other cars so that if you backed up or went forward, your tires were punctured. Who here is doing the right thing? The people working honestly in the fields or the people shouting dirty words from the picket line?"

Several days later, I drove out to see one of Pandol's labor camps. Like all the growers in Delano, he keeps his workers segregated—the Mexicans in one camp; the Filipinos in another; Puerto Ricans in a third. "They all eat different things," Pandol explained. "It's easier this way. We deduct two dollars a day and furnish camps and cooks."

"Bedding?" I asked.

"No blankets, no pillow," he answered. "They steal them."

I asked how he could be sure that his men, even though they stayed on the job, did not favor the NFWA.

"My men made their position clear by staying on the job," he answered.

Persisting, I asked if the growers might have been able to undercut criticism by holding a secret-ballot election which conceivably could have upheld their contention that their workers did not support the NFWA.

"When my people are unhappy, they come see me," Pandol insisted. "This isn't a strike, it's a revolution."

"But what about an election?"

"This is a ranch, not a voting booth," he said. "We can't have a ballot every morning, the X's go to work, the Y's stay home."

There the subject was dropped.

TEN

Among the growers, there was little inclination to take their case to the public. "We had a crop to harvest," Bruno Dispoto told me. "Telling our story was secondary. And anyway, people just weren't buying the good-guy grower story." For a short while, after a number of their most imprudent statements were released to the press, the growers did agree to channel all their comments on the strike through a spokesman of the Agricultural Labor Bureau, who set up shop in the Stardust Motel. But the tenor of the growers' pronouncements changed, if at all, imperceptibly. In one press release, the spokesman noted that only two major agricultural employers had recognized unions in the past five years. "At the rate of two organizations each five years," he added with satisfaction, "agriculture will be unionized sometime in the twenty-first century."

Thus, almost by default, the task of justifying Delano to the world fell to the people of the town. Shortly after the strike started, a group of townspeople banded together in an organization called Citizens for Facts from Delano. Its main function was to buff the image of the town, which had been, they thought, tarnished with malice aforethought by Chavez and the NFWA. Several days after I arrived in Delano, I stopped in at the Citizens for Facts office on Main Street to pick up some of their literature. In an issue of *The Truth—La Verdad*, I discovered a verse which, although it did not scan, accurately summed up the feelings of the organization's members:

Citizens for Facts was formed
By ladies with nothing to do,
This may have been your first thought,
But, Chavez, it was because of you.

The major thrust of the Citizens for Facts campaign was a fusillade of leaflets, broadsides, pamphlets, posters, reprints, and letters-to-the-editor suggesting obscure and tortuous links between Cesar Chavez and something which after a few weeks in Delano even I came to call "the Communist conspiracy." "Agriculture is the very foundation of our nation," one leaflet informed me. "Weaken our agriculture and our entire structure would give way and weaken and crumble. There is no doubt there are outside influences that would like to see this happen." In the Delano *Record,* a twice-weekly newspaper which is the most consistent trumpeter of grower virtues, Citizens for Facts briefed local residents planning trips abroad on how to parry foreigners when the subject of Delano was brought up. "NFWA SAYS: 'We are the true farm worker,'" one fact sheet said. "FACTS ARE: Chavez and his cohorts have imported the long-haired kooks, professional loafers, winos and dregs of society to carry their *Huelga* banners. The true farm workers are in the fields working."

Outside the novels of Mary McCarthy, I had never heard the name of Leon Trotsky invoked so often. (One mystery I was never able to clear up was how the townspeople had bypassed Marx, Lenin, and Stalin in favor of Trotsky as the black angel of the NFWA.) After Trotsky

and Chavez, the most prominent figure in the local demonology was Chavez's mentor in the CSO, Saul Alinsky.
It was difficult to engage anyone in conversation on the
East Side without being told that Alinsky was a "well-
known radical," a phrase which in Delano took on overtones of criminal syndicalism. "Most of these people don't
know who the hell Alinsky is," a Valley newspaperman
close to the Delano situation told me. "All they know is
that he's got a name like a bomb thrower."

For the most part, the townspeople of Delano were far
more accessible then either the growers or the NFWA.
They seemed to have a compulsion to talk about the strike,
and wherever I met them, in the street, in their offices, at
their homes, they unburdened themselves without prodding. Perhaps their readiness to talk could be traced to
their ambivalent position in Delano's social structure.
They are more equal than the Filipinos and the Mexicans
on the West Side, but until the strike was underway they
were never really accepted socially by the growers. I ques-
tioned Joe Hochschild, Delano's mayor, on this point, and
he reluctantly concurred that there had never been a
strong relationship between the growers and the town.
"The Slavs are like the Mexicans," he said. "They have a
heritage problem. They stay among their own, like the
Mexicans do. Even people who were born here, right here
in Delano, they still speak with a Yugoslavian accent. But
one thing the strike has done is bring the Slavs closer to
the city people."

The reason, of course, is that the townspeople, like
papal courtiers more Catholic than the Pope, were more
violently antipathetic to Chavez than the growers most directly affected by him. They struggled to maintain their

"Your miserable boss says we're Communists"

"Humble, happy, built close to the ground . . ."

(Opposite) The Grapes of Delano

Main Street, Delano, Kern County, California

"Our biggest mistake was in thinking Chavez was just another dumb Mex"

Cesar Chavez at the NFWA Camp

Rev. James Drake of the California Migrant Ministry outside NFWA headquarters

Capt. Al Espinosa, the ranking Mexican-American on the Delano Police Force

Saul Alinsky

Fred Ross

Jack Pandol: "All Chavez is trying to do is replace my power structure with his"

The strike vigil outside DiGiorgio's Sierra Vista Ranch

Chavez giving counsel inside NFWA headquarters

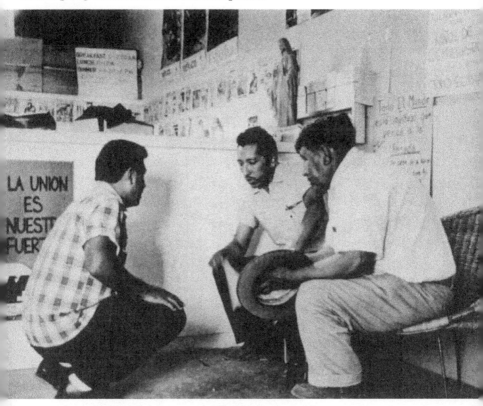

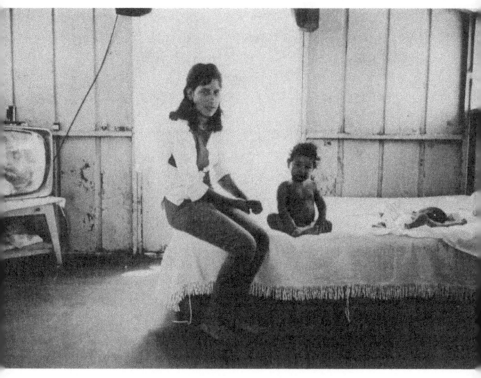

A farmworker's family housing unit, Tulare County, California

The *campesinos*

The march to Sacramento

Teamster (*right*) campaigning for votes before DiGiorgio election

Election day, Sierra Vista Ranch

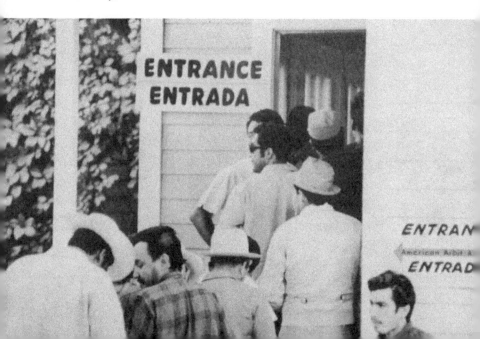

Cesar and Helen Chavez singing *Nosotros Venceremos* the night before the election

"It is not the beginning of the end; it is not even the end of the beginning"

All photographs by Ted Streshinsky

impartiality—"Everyone's got a right to join a union," was a sentence heard in the first moments of any conversation conducted in Delano—but it gave way to unalloyed loathing before the suggestion of the NFWA that Delano might not be the happiest little town in America. Their answers to these charges served to make them only more beleaguered and isolated, trapped in a situation from which they could not extricate themselves. I cite three examples.

Police Chief James C. Ailes is a lean, hawk-faced Nebraskan who was a captain in the Seaside police department in Monterey County before being appointed to his present post. He seemed ill at ease when I began talking to him in his office, and to break the ice I mentioned a fatal accident outside my house in Los Angeles a few days before. The victim was a young Hollywood actor whose family lived in Delano. "I heard that boy was incinerated," Chief Ailes said. "Driving a Volkswagen. That car's a death trap. My son wanted one and I said, 'No, sir, you get yourself a secondhand Pontiac or Chevvy, some good car.'" He shook his head slowly. "I've seen too many accidents in my time. I see one now, and I'm not on duty, I don't even stop, so long as there's someone there. I remember one. A Marine pilot. Just dove straight into the ground. Mush, that's what he was, nothing but mush. Couldn't find enough of him to scrape into a jelly jar."

His reserve vanished and I brought the subject around to the strike. "We tried right from the start to keep neutral," Chief Ailes said. "But so far as the NFWA is concerned, if you're not for them, you're against them. So we're in the wrong, no matter what." To improve the situation, the Delano police force changed the color of its uniforms to blue from the suntans and O.D. twills it had previously worn. "In the first place, I think a policeman should be in blue," Ailes said. "But there were other reasons. The Highway Patrol and the Kern County and Tulare County sheriff's departments all wore the same kind of uniforms we did. So no matter what happened, even if it happened ten miles outside town, the NFWA crowd still blamed the Delano cops. By changing, we could be identified. We were the ones wearing the blue. If there was an incident, and the officer wasn't wearing blue, well, they couldn't blame us."

I asked what he thought of the outsiders who had flocked to Chavez's support. "It's difficult for me to see how a college graduate or a preacher can be associated with some of the things this crowd's been saying," he said. "They're outsiders coming into a community that's been peaceful for years. When you get clergymen coming in here on the pretext of an unbiased investigation and you meet with them at 11 a.m. and they've already sent out a press release distorting what hasn't even been said yet, well, I just can't understand that. Excuse me, but I just can't. Look, these people held a rally in Ellington Park and they said that two, three thousand people showed up. We did a head count and I know that only 500, maybe 550 were there. And of that 550, I bet 129 were juveniles. Hell, the farm workers were out in the fields working.

"These churches, they say they're concerned with the migrants. But you know what they're doing? They're trying to differentiate between the migrants. Hell, you take old man Caratan [one of the largest Delano growers]. They say he's worth $27 million, $27 *million*. Well, he's a migrant. He migrated here from Yugoslavia. But he made it. He's no different from the Mexican except for that. But he's still out here working every day, laying pipe and the like. Well, just because a man's successful he shouldn't be treated any different from the man who isn't. Hell, I'm a migrant. I migrated here from Nebraska. You just can't differentiate.

"You know, outside of kicking hell out of the Indians, this has been a pretty good old country. It's a free country. Anybody can do anything he wants. Well, these people start knocking this free enterprise, I suggest they go somewhere else and be happy."

I asked Chief Ailes what he, as a neutral, thought of a farm workers' union. He pondered his answer. "If somebody, if some union moves in and takes over the food industry," he said finally, "then they might as well tell old Lyndon Johnson to go back to Texas. There's no way this country can survive if that happens."

Joe Hochschild, the mayor of Delano, is a short, earnest, amiable man who was born, as was I, in Hartford, Connecticut, a coincidence that augmented his already generous fund of Rotarian fellowship. The mayor's job is largely ceremonial ("I wouldn't say that, but I guess you would," he said somewhat reproachfully); Delano is run by a salaried city manager, and the mayor, who is a city councilman, is elected by the other four members of the council to chair their meetings. A councilman's salary is only $150 a month, and so they all have full-time jobs. I met Hochschild at The Press, a commercial printing shop he owns on Delano's East Side. He was wearing blue coveralls and his hands were covered with printer's ink. There were a couple of presses in the back of the shop, and on the counter, sample wedding invitations and vespers' announcements. On the bulletin board was a printed announcement: "NOW YOUR TOWN CAN HAVE A PROFESSIONAL RIOT. No more 'amateur' demonstrations. NAME YOUR CAUSE. WE WILL DEMONSTRATE. Riot kits. Press 'service.' We specialize in hand-picked hoodlums who can't speak English. All have passed the go-limp test."

We drove from his office across the freeway to a truck stop called the Cave Inn, on Highway 99, where we ordered coffee. "First of all," he said, "I want to be proud of my town. My boy is at Fresno State and I told him to tell people there that Delano is a nice town to live in. It's a friendly, easy place. People have come to town and the very first thing they do is attack us. Do they come to the city council, do they go to the churches, do they see our schools? No. But they say our schools are discriminatory and our churches aren't doing the job. How can they say that? They haven't been here long enough to drink the water. All they want to do is threaten. All they want to do is call names. They want to break down the structure of the schools and churches. If the workers want to strike, okay, strike. But what has this to do with the high school, the churches, the city council? And anyway, the workers weren't on strike. The people on the picket line were kids who wanted to spend a weekend screaming. I don't want to sound derogatory, but if all the workers had gone on strike, Chavez would have won. The growers would have had to give in. But they didn't. What does Chavez do? He kicks us in the ass, stabs us in the back, then wants us to play ball with him. That's some ball game."

Al Espinosa is a heavy-set Mexican-American with dark, nervous eyes who is a captain in the Delano police department. A few years ago he was fired from the police force and subsequently reinstated through pressure applied by, among others, the CSO. Espinosa also moonlights as a labor contractor. He is keenly aware of his role as a member of Delano's Mexican-American establishment. It is for these latter two functions that he has come under attack by the NFWA, which believes that Delano's Mexican-American leaders mirror the wishes of the Anglo hierarchy far more than they do the needs of the field workers west of the freeway. I spoke to Espinosa one morning in his office at the police station. There was a coiled rattlesnake ashtray on his desk, and a newspaper cartoon under the glass desk cover showing Hubert Humphrey in military battle dress and Robert Kennedy embraced by a liberal siren holding a draft card. The cartoon's caption was, "Could I trouble you for a match, Hubert?"

I asked Espinosa if, as a Mexican-American, he didn't feel a certain ambivalence about the strike. His arm flailed the air as he vigorously denied any uncertainty about his position. "Those NFWA people are trying to tear down the prestige of my office," he said angrily. "They're trying to make me a hate object. Now they're singling out the Mexican-American leaders who have a position in this city, as hate objects. The schools, the doctors, the growers, everyone who is opposed to them, is a hate object. I abhor those SNCC Anglos coming in here to teach the Mexicans how to be civilized and nonviolent. My people are by nature nonviolent and we don't need Anglos to teach us non-violence. And I don't point my finger at the Anglos. I point it at Cesar Chavez. He's selling his people short. If he had worked with the leaders of the Mexican-American community, he probably would have forged a compromise."

I suggested that as a labor contractor he might not be altogether acceptable as a broker between the growers and the NFWA, since Chavez regards contractors as lackeys of the ranchers, bearing a large part of the responsibility for the continued poverty of the migrants. "They say I've got an interest in this strike," he challenged, his voice rising, "an interest in seeing the union get beat. What's the matter with being a contractor? There's thousands of labor contractors in California. They've got families, they've got plans for the future, a better education for their kids, a better car and house. If a man comes along in a dictatorial fashion and says, 'This is wrong,' then I'm against it. You might as well do away with farm workers as well. Contracting is a business like any other business, the restaurant business or the bakery business."

I replied that he was dealing with men, not doughnuts. "Any business is run under the same principles," he said. "If a contractor realizes a profit, that means he's taking good care of his people."

The equation escaped me, but I did not press the point. I asked if he thought the strike had done irreparable damage to Delano. "The scars will never heal," he answered ominously. "After this little thing is over with, the Mexican-American leaders are going to retaliate against these militants. They've got influence right up to the governor. They're not going to forget someone called them Judas. These people are sophisticated. They've got education and breeding and they're going to get back."

With feelings running in this direction, it took only a short inductive leap for the townspeople of Delano to conclude that anyone connected with the NFWA was a Communist dupe or worse. In one reprint I picked up at the Citizens for Facts office, the Reverend Wayne C. Hartmire, director of the California Migrant Ministry, was identified as a "former convict" because he had been arrested on a civil-rights march. Many of the volunteers had been involved with the Free Speech Movement at Berkeley and were sympathetic to, when not actually members of, CORE, SNCC, and the Students for a Democratic Society; in Delano, such associations were tantamount to taking instructions from Peking. Others in fact did belong to the W. E. B. DuBois clubs and the Progressive Labor Party. Luis Valdez, one of Chavez's top aides, had traveled in Cuba under the auspices of the Castro government, and Alex Hoffman, the NFWA's attorney, had been cited by the California State Senate Report on Un-American activities at Berkeley as having "made no effort to conceal his Marxist convictions."

So much was made on the East Side of Valdez and Hoffman that one day I asked Chavez if he thought he could blunt the criticism by getting rid of his most radical followers. "There's not that many," he replied. "And if we did, I'm afraid people would start thinking they'd have to take a loyalty oath just to help us." Chavez was most impressively supported on this stand by the Catholic Bishop of Stockton, the most Reverend Hugh Donohoe. "Whenever there is a weakness in our society, it behooves the supposed to disappear just because the Communists appear on the scene? Of course not. We should remedy the situation so that Communists cannot exploit it."

And yet it was not necessarily a symptom of paranoia to have ambivalent feelings about the volunteers. Some—the Migrant Ministry, the professional SNCC and CORE people—were indispensable to Chavez in organizing picket lines, raising money, and unsnarling the NFWA's administration. But to get the indispensables, for no one knew who they were when they checked into Delano for the first time, Chavez had to put up with countless rejects and romantics, the eternally young who tended to confuse their own problems with the problems of mankind and for whom the age of thirty was a passport into a land of disillusion and dread. This was especially true by the time I arrived in Delano. After nearly a year, a kind of strike bureaucracy had been set in motion, and as routine took over, its participants became suffused with their own importance. "The workers don't completely know what's going on," one hefty young girl informed me. Several days later, this same girl elbowed me aside as I was talking to Alex Hoffman. "Private business," she said peremptorily. The private business was whether to put a five-cent or an airmail stamp on a letter to San Francisco.

For many, Delano was not the first cause nor would it be the last. One evening I talked with a striking redheaded girl in her mid-twenties who had previously been in Mississippi with SNCC. She seemed to accept the fact that the Mexicans would one day no longer need her, as the Negroes no longer wanted her in the South. I wondered what she would do when she was older and disenchantment had set in. And then she said, "Maybe I'll organize the middle class."

Scarcely an evening went by that the volunteers did not gather in a West Side bar called People's to drink beer and play pool on three threadbare old tables. In the jukebox there was a strike song called "El Corrido de Delano," which I heard only once in the three weeks I was in town, and that when I played it. Behind the bar was a cartoon depicting the DiGiorgio ranch—the largest in Delano—as an octopus. The irony that the octopus in Frank Norris's famed muckraking novel of the same name was the Southern Pacific Railroad, and the growers its victims, was completely lost on the volunteers. The newer volunteers, in fact, were appallingly ignorant about California, the Valley, and the growers. Nowhere was this more apparent than in *El Malcriado,* the strikers' newspaper, which has as little regard for fact as a Citizens for Facts broadsheet. In the first issue I read, I saw an item about women being "used as bribes, offered to male employees as a reward" for a vote against the NFWA. (Chavez likes to claim disingenuously that *El Malcriado* is a separate corporation with no ties to the NFWA, but it is published by volunteers from a back room at NFWA headquarters.) Instead of knowing their enemies, a number of the volunteers whom I met had developed colorful notions about them. One girl said that she had never been on the East Side, and when I asked why, she said, "They won't let me." To others it came as a revelation when I told them that the land had been arid before water was pumped in and that a large number of the growers were Yugoslavian. One asked me if I had actually met any growers, and when I said that often they were easier to see than the NFWA, she replied, "Well, growers have got people to do their work for them."

However East Side Delano raged at the volunteers, it still reserved its purest vitriol for the clergy who came to town in support of the NFWA. What particularly infuriated Delano was the clergy's insistence that the situation involved not simply a labor dispute but a moral issue. The outside clergy maintained that their presence in Delano was necessary because the local churchmen, by remaining neutral, had by their silence cast in with the growers. All over California, Catholic, Protestant, and Jewish clergymen collected food and money for the strikers, walked in their marches, and, when they came to Delano, were arrested on the picket lines. In its enthusiasm, the Catholic archdiocese of San Francisco even indulged in a kind of *realpolitik* with strong overtones of blackmail; in a letter to the owner of the Beaulieu Vineyards, the archdiocese suggested that since she was the major supplier of altar wines to the churches of San Francisco, it behooved her to recognize the NFWA.

Delano's reaction to the clergy's campaign was predictable. One grower, Martin Zaninovich, recommended that ranchers cut off their financial support to the churches because of "these radical theories they are attempting to force upon us." The pastor of the First Baptist Church of Delano, Dr. Floyd W. Reed, saw something ominous in the fact that the NFWA had purchased four automobile tires with a credit card belonging to the California Migrant Ministry. "No moral issue is involved," Dr. Reed said. "Somebody is going to be a winner in this dispute, and if we are allied with the winners, the losers will have no respect for us." Dr. Reed also wondered how "the migrant ministers are able to demonstrate moral standards anywhere when the car they drive is laden with empty beer cans." In reply, the Reverend Wayne C. Hartmire, director of the Migrant Ministry, said that he did not consider beer drinking a primary ethical issue of the day.

Of all the local clergymen, the one most frequently mentioned as a defender of the town is the Reverend R. B. Moore, pastor of St. Paul's Baptist Church and the only Negro in the Delano Kiwanis Club. I visited the Reverend Moore late one Saturday afternoon at his home next door to his church on the West Side of Delano. The television set was on and all during our conversation he kept half an eye peeled on an old Herbert Marshall movie on "TV Spectacular" out of Bakersfield. I asked the Reverend Moore what he thought about the strikers. "A hog grunts because it's his nature to grunt," he replied enigmatically, and when I asked him to explain, he said, "There's a number of people in Delano who joined the pickets not because they are poor or hungry but because it's just their nature to grunt." I wondered if he included the Migrant Ministry in this category. It was several moments before he answered. "They came to town investigating and went first to the grievance committee," he said. "Folks with a crying towel is the wrong people to see. And that bunch wasn't any kind of Christian I know. If they held a prayer meeting or any kind of religious service, I haven't heard of it. They're more concerned with a man's income than they are with his soul. They're not working *for* the people, they're working *on* the people."

The Reverend Moore once ran for the Delano City Council and lost. "My friends let me know they weren't going to allow me to become city property when I was so needed in the ministry," he explains. He deeply resents the NFWA accusation that there is discrimination or poverty in Delano. "Why, we got a regular little United Nations here in Delano," he said. "Ask anyone in Bakersfield. We got Mexicans on the police force and we got a Negro beautician in a beauty parlor. And if Chavez and that striking bunch says there's so many poor people in Delano, why didn't they come and pick up the old clothes I keep in my garage? They called me once and said there was poor people in town if I'd just go out and look. And I said to them, 'Safeway doesn't go out and solicit business. People who want food go there and buy.' They want my clothes, they can come here and pick 'em up. They're right here for the asking. But no one came."

It was difficult for me to realize, however, just how embattled Delano was until I attended a Citizens for Facts meeting. The meeting was held in the Delano Women's Club. There were about seventy-five people in the room, mostly older men and women, all Anglo save for perhaps half a dozen Mexicans and Filipinos. On a table there was a pot of coffee and pitchers of Kool-Aid. The main topic on the agenda that night was an upcoming investigation of the Delano situation by the California Senate Fact-Finding Committee for Agriculture. After a brief address by one of the senators on the committee, Kern County Democrat Walter Stiern, the meeting was thrown open to the floor.

"Senator," someone asked, "how do you get the workers to testify? I'm speaking of the farm worker who is not a member of a union and doesn't want to join. He might not want to speak."

"You think he'll feel intimidated?" Senator Stiern asked. "You're darn right that's what I mean." There was a murmur of assent from the rest of the audience.

To prove the point, Jack Pandol began to play a tape recording of conversations he had with nonstrikers. "Did they threaten you?" Pandol's voice asked.

A woman answered to the accompaniment of squalling children in the background. "The only threat this guy said was that we would never have a job if they won. That if we did want to work, we would have to come on our knees, to crawl to them and ask for a job."

Pandol asked the nature of the threat. "This guy said, 'You better not sign that card because it's going to be pretty hard for you,'" the woman replied. "I said, 'Are you threatening me?' and he said, 'Oh, no, I'm just telling you.'"

When Pandol switched off the tape, a grower's wife passed through the audience handing out reprints of an article entitled "Communist Wrath in Delano," which had been published in the John Birch Society magazine, *American Opinion*. (I learned later that the Birch reprint had been passed out to workers in the fields and also sent to a number of members of the California legislature.) A man called Loren Juday, who works in the Citizens for Facts office, then got up and said, "We sent a letter to President Johnson and asked why we are fighting Communists all over the world and not fighting it right here in Delano." He sat down to rousing applause. The next speaker was Richard Myer, personnel director at the DiGiorgio ranch. "I can assure you one thing," Myer said. "As long as I'm working for DiGiorgio, we won't capitulate. And if we do, *I'll* quit."

"Did you see that Father Salandini taking pictures on the picket line?" someone asked. "He was telling them, 'We got your picture.' And him a priest in the Catholic Church."

"He's no priest in the Catholic Church I know," someone else answered.

"Maybe he's an Episcopalian in disguise," a third added.

"Chavez only claims he's got a union because it sounds good," Pandol said.

"He doesn't want a union, Jack, he wants a social revolution."

At this point, there was a motion about what insignia members of Citizens for Facts should wear at the state senate hearing.

"Let's wear the American flag," a woman in the audience volunteered.

"That's right, not some Trotsky flag. Leave that to Chavez."

The motion for the American flag was referred to committee.

ELEVEN

Three months after the strike began, Chavez found the stratagem to focus nationwide attention on Delano. The tactic was economic boycott.

Though grapes might not seem to lend themselves to boycott, the two biggest ranches in Delano did. The DiGiorgio Corporation, with 4,400 acres in Delano, and Schenley Industries, Inc., with 3,350 acres, were absentee landlords only minimally interested in farming. Less than ten percent of DiGiorgio's $232 million annual revenues came from farming; the bulk came from the processing and sale of canned goods. Similarly, only a fraction of Schenley's $500 million annual sales, mostly in distilled spirits, derived from its farming properties. For both companies, the profits from agriculture were marginal, if any; DiGiorgio's farming operation, for example, has lost money three out of the five preceding years.

The situation of both companies appealed to Chavez. No other ranches in Delano could afford him the means to tell the NFWA's story so effectively. Both DiGiorgio and Schenley distributed their products through outlets across the nation. Both had scores of contracts with other unions that they could not afford to compromise by behaving cavalierly with the NFWA. In addition, it was unlikely that either company wanted to jeopardize its consumer sales on behalf of an agricultural operation that barely paid its way. Early in December, Chavez's boycott plans were given a boost when the AFL-CIO convention in San Francisco, after some assiduous backstage lobbying for the NFWA, passed a resolution supporting the grape strike. The next day, Walter Reuther himself came to Delano to bestow the AFL-CIO's official blessing. The town was in an ugly mood. Outside the Filipino Hall on the West Side, a fight nearly broke out between strikers and townspeople carrying placards reading, "You Are Not Welcome Here, Mr. Reuther," and "We Can Take Care of Our Own Problems." The mayor of Delano arranged a secret meeting between Reuther and a contingent of local growers, but it broke up with both sides intractable. "We will put the full support of organized labor behind your boycott and this is a powerful economic weapon," Reuther told the strikers. "You are making history here and we will march here together, we will fight here together, and we will win here together."

From the beginning, Chavez decided to concentrate the boycott on Schenley. "It was a simple decision," he told me one day. "In the first place, booze is easier to boycott. And then it is usually the man who goes to the liquor store and he's more sympathetic to labor as a rule than his wife." From an atlas, Chavez picked thirteen major cities across the United States as boycott centers, and then raised a boycott staff, all under twenty-five, from workers and volunteers who had impressed him on the picket line. They left Delano penniless and hitchhiked or rode the rails to the various cities where they were to set up shop. Chavez gave the boycott staff no money, both out of necessity and to prove a theory. He reasoned that if a person could not put his hands on enough money to maintain himself on a subsistence level, then he would be of little use raising money for the boycott and setting up an organization. In most cities, the boycott staffers went to union locals and begged room, board, an office, a telephone, and whatever help was available. Across the country, they recruited some 10,000 people to pass out leaflets or to telephone neighbors, friends, churches, and stores, urging support of the boycott. (In Los Angeles, I came out of a supermarket one day to find, stuck under the windshield wiper of my car, a leaflet that said: "Steve Allen and the Los Angeles friends of the grape strikers urge you not to buy (1) Schenley Products (2) Delano grapes." A few days later, the supermarket put up a sign: "We do not handle Delano grapes.")

The staffers were seldom at a loss for ingenuity. In Boston, one staged a Boston Grape Party. He bought several lugs of Delano grapes, organized a march, and paraded his charges through town to the waterfront where, with attendant publicity, the grapes were dumped into Massachusetts Bay. In New York, another talked the Transport Workers Union into printing and passing out one million boycott leaflets in the city's subways. In all, fifty million leaflets were distributed throughout the country.

In Delano, the NFWA even arranged to boycott the freight-car loads of table grapes that rolled out of town by rail to markets around the nation. Contacting SNCC and CORE, Chavez rounded up a cadre of volunteers who had ridden the rails before. "We'd slip them on the trains right here in Delano," he told me. "We'd cover the yard with pickets and create a big scene, maybe start a fight or something, and then when everyone was looking the other way, they'd hop on the train. Sometimes a train would make six or seven stops, and at each one our people would slip off and contact our local organization to tell them a load of Delano grapes was in town. The local people would then set up the pickets." One volunteer team rode the rods with a load of grapes all the way from Delano to Hoboken, New Jersey. Another was apprehended by a railroad employee as their train was crossing one of the snow-covered Western mountain ranges. Telling them they would freeze to death if they stayed on the train, the railroad man bought them bus tickets to the first stop on the other side of the mountains, where he told them they could get back on board. He was a good union man, he said, and this was his contribution to the Delano strike. "We even had girl volunteers who wanted to ride the rails," Chavez told me. "But I wouldn't let them. They were really upset."

Though the economic effects of the boycott were negligible (despite the grandiose claims of the NFWA), the adverse publicity began to worry executives of both Schenley and DiGiorgio. Chavez was well aware of their concern, as secret information was constantly passed to him from informants inside both companies. The NFWA's man at Schenley was a disgruntled employee passed over for promotion, but the identity of the DiGiorgio informant was unknown. He would neither meet with the NFWA nor talk to the union over the telephone. His information came by mail to a postal box in Delano, and the NFWA got in touch with him in the same way. Fully cognizant of the situation within both companies, Chavez decided to publicize the boycott even further.

He chose to do it by means of a *peregrinación,* or pilgrimage, from Delano to the state capital at Sacramento.

The notion was first born shortly after the strike started, when Schenley ranch crews sprayed pickets with insecticides and fertilizer. Outraged, some NFWA members proposed that five striking families make a protest pilgrimage across the country from Delano to Schenley's corporate headquarters in New York. The march to New York was clearly unfeasible, but the idea of a *peregrinación* stuck. Chavez was well aware of the emotional impact of the Selma civil-rights march in the South, and after much discussion it was decided that the march should terminate on Easter Sunday at the steps of the capitol building in Sacramento. The choice of Sacramento was calculated. Up to that point, both the state legislature and the then governor, Edmund G. ("Pat") Brown, had been indifferent to the strike. Early in the walkout, when Pat Brown was asked if he intended to take any action, he had replied, "What can a governor do to end a strike?" A *peregrinación* would not only embarrass Schenley and DiGiorgio but also put pressure on Pat Brown.

Late in February, the NFWA began signing up marchers for the 250-mile hike to Sacramento. Only a limited number of pickets were allowed to sign on, since picketing and the operation of the nursery school, clinic, store, soup kitchen, and NFWA office in Delano had to continue. Of the one hundred names on the initial list, doctors struck off all those with diabetes, bad feet, high blood pressure, and sick wives at home. The rest received their assignments, some to drive the luggage and toilet trucks, others to act as advance men, visiting towns ahead of the marchers, arranging meals, halls for meetings, places to sleep.

The *peregrinación* was scheduled to begin on March 17, but it very nearly did not make it out of Delano. "We knew the march was coming up," Chief Ailes told me. "There was a report about it in *Newsweek* magazine. They just acted as if nothing was going to happen, but we were monitoring their radios, just like they were monitoring ours, and we heard them asking for bedding, tents, food, stuff like that." A day or so before the start, Chief Ailes said, Alex Hoffman told him that the marchers were going to walk down Albany Street, which is the city line, and then on out of town. But on March 17, the marchers, with Chavez leading them, changed their plans and prepared to walk through the center of Delano. "They didn't have no permit to do that," Chief Ailes said. Immediately a line of police blocked their route of march. So many reporters and television cameramen were on the scene that Ailes and Delano's city manager, Louis Shepard, decided to avoid an incident and let the marchers go through town. "They wanted us to arrest them," Chief Ailes said. "But that was one time we just lucked out. They were all down on their knees with their priests saying all their words and what not. It would have made them look good if we arrested them with all that press and TV there. No, I got to say we just lucked out."

For twenty-five days, the marchers straggled up through the Valley behind the banner of the Virgin of Gaudalupe, who symbolized the Mexico of the poor and the humble. The first night, when they stopped to rest, one of the marchers discovered a seven-year-old boy who had skipped school, eluded his mother, and was intent on trekking to Sacramento. He was reluctantly sent home, and sixty-seven marched on. Every night, feet were soaked and blisters treated. Peggy McGivern, the NFWA's nurse, lanced so many blisters that one night she dreamed that one burst and its serum gushed out in a tidal wave, engulf-ing her. At each town, the ranks of the marchers swelled as farm workers joined the *peregrinación* for a mile or an hour or even a whole day. Scores of new members signed with the NFWA, and their families gave the marchers rosaries, mass cards, fruit, tea, and food. In the evening, rallies were held which were like religious revivals. At each rally, the NFWA's plan of Delano was read: "We are suffering . . . We shall unite . . . We shall strike . . . We shall overcome . . . Our pilgrimage is the match that will light our cause for all farm workers to see what is happen-ing here, so that they may do as we have done."

To the delight of the rally audiences, El Teatro Campe-sino (The Farm Workers' Theater, an adjunct of the NFWA set up to raise money and to publicize the strike throughout the state) nightly performed broad, neo-Brechtian skits about *esquiroles* (scabs), *contratistas* (contractors), *patroncitos* (growers), and *huelguistas* (strikers). The most successful playlet involved the DiGi-orgio Corporation.

"When the time for the Teatro came," says Luis Valdez, the group's founder and director, "the DiGiorgio character —complete with sign, dark glasses, and cigar—leaped onto the truck used as a stage for the rallies and was booed and reviled by the audience. Threatening them with the loss of their jobs, blackballing, and deportation, 'DiGior-gio' blustered and guffawed his way through all the boo-ing, and announced that his old school buddy, the gover-nor, was coming to speak to them that same night, and in Spanish. At this point, a car with a siren and loudspeaker drove up behind the audience, honking and moving to-ward the platform. An authoritative voice commanded the workers to move out of the way, and the outside rally was momentarily halted as 'Governor Brown' was pulled out of the car by his cronies and pushed on to the stage.

" 'No huelga,' they exhorted, 'just say *no huelga.*'

" 'And *no boycoteo,*' insisted DiGiorgio.

"The governor not only spoke Spanish, he spoke so ardently that he turned into a Mexican. This is the turning point of the *acto.* DiGiorgio and his friends were forced to drag the metamorphosed governor off the stage as he shouted, '*Huelga, huelga.*' "

Easter Sunday, the marchers paraded into Sacramento. I was standing on the balcony of the capitol building and it was like watching newsreels of de Gaulle marching into Paris in 1944. Below, on the mall, thousands of people were cheering and weeping and waving Mexican flags. "Clear away the dignitaries," a Spanish-accented voice commanded over the loudspeaker. "Clear away the dignitaries. The platform is reserved for the *originales*"—the fifty-seven marchers who had walked the entire distance between Delano and Sacramento. The villain of the day was neither Schenley nor DiGiorgio but Pat Brown. The governor had declined to meet with the strikers, saying that he had a previous engagement to spend the holiday with his family. With ill-concealed delight, the NFWA announced that the setting for the governor's family holiday was the Palm Springs home of Frank Sinatra.

As the afternoon wore on, it started to rain and the excitement began to ebb. Ponderousness replaced the throbbing revivalist flavor of the march. Speech followed interminable speech, each rendered in both Spanish and English. Priests and ministers compared the *peregrinación* with the Passion, rabbis the Passion with Passover. If

Passover was a mystery to the *campesinos*, it was less so than the peroration delivered by the director of the Migrant Ministry, the Reverend Hartmire, who chose as his text relevant passages from the works of Albert Camus. All that saved the day was the residual excitement from an announcement made a few days before: Schenley had capitulated.

Less than a month before, Schenley had stated categorically that it would not recognize the NFWA. What troubled the company was the fear of stockholder reaction if it recognized a union so ardently supported by the radical left, in particular Students for a Democratic Society and the W. E. B. DuBois clubs. The publicity generated by the boycott undermined the company's determination. Clergymen denounced Schenley from the pulpit, and letters of protest poured in from over forty states. Otherwise completely organized, the company began to feel pressure from the unions with which it had contracts. The Teamsters refused to cross an NFWA picket line outside the warehouse of Schenley's major distributor in San Francisco and threatened to stop serving a supermarket chain that carried Schenley products.

Clearly up against it, Schenley retained Sidney Korshak, a Los Angeles attorney, to get the company out of its corner. Korshak's negotiations were proceeding nowhere when a piece of misinformation brought matters to a head. The misinformation arrived via Herman "Blackie" Leavitt, the head of the Bartenders' Union in Los Angeles. Not long before, the NFWA had asked Leavitt to help the strike by declaring a bartenders' boycott on Schenley products. Leavitt refused, but after some persuasion reluctantly agreed to help the NFWA by picking up the cost of a mailing. In the telling, however, the story got turned around, and word filtered back to Korshak that the bartenders were about to boycott Schenley products. The threat of a boycott was the lever that Korshak sought. He contacted Leavitt and asked him not to do anything for a while. "Since I wasn't doing anything anyway," Leavitt told a friend, "it was easy to agree to keep on doing nothing."

Korshak next got in touch with Lewis Solon Rosensteil, then Schenley's seventy-five-year-old board chairman and chief stockholder. Noted for his contentiousness, Rosensteil had for years feuded with the liquor industry over its marketing practices and more recently had spent a large part of his time in court fighting with, among others, his estranged fourth wife, his daughter, one of his lawyers, and his neighbors in Greenwich, Connecticut. Korshak told Rosensteil about the rumors (false) of the bartenders' boycott. The strike, however, did not loom as large in Rosensteil's thinking as it did in Cesar Chavez's or in the minds of the growers of Delano, and Korshak had to bring him up to date. When informed that only 200 grape pickers were involved, Rosensteil told Korshak that he was not a farmer but was in the liquor business, and ordered him to sell the Schenley properties in Delano. As an alternative, Korshak suggested that Schenley could avoid the bartenders' boycott by recognizing the NFWA, thus coming out of the dispute with its tarnished image buffed up. Rosensteil finally agreed and gave Korshak carte blanche in settling the strike. So a bartenders' boycott that was never even contemplated brought Schenley in line, and, on April 6, an agreement was signed that left the NFWA free to concentrate its attack on DiGiorgio.

TWELVE

Unlike Schenley, which was relatively new to its role as grower, DiGiorgio had long been a reigning power in California agriculture. The company was founded by a Sicilian immigrant, Joseph DiGiorgio, who as a fourteen-year-old boy landed in New York in 1888 with fifty cents to his name. He found work with a fruit jobber at $8 a week, learned the business so well that before he was twenty he was able to borrow $700 from a fellow Sicilian to set himself up as a fruit importer in Baltimore. The business prospered. He borrowed an additional $5,000 in working capital from the Maryland National Bank, repaid the loan, and by the time he was twenty-one, was sitting on the bank's board of directors. From Baltimore, his vistas widened. He chartered a fleet of twenty-nine ships to carry his produce to Europe, Canada, and ports around the United States, and set up fruit auctions in Baltimore, Pittsburgh, and New York. In California, he bought the accounts of the Earl Fruit Company, the oldest shipping concern of its kind in the country. Through Earl, he bankrolled a number of California growers with loans, then decided to become a grower himself. As a start, in 1915, he picked up 2,000 acres near Arvin and another 2,000 in Delano, never paying more than $90 an acre. The land was leveled, wells were dug, and the fields were laid out in rows of vines and fruit trees. Cactus and sagebrush gave way to grapes and plums, and the successful harvests brought new coolers, packing sheds, and railroad spurs.

Along with his land, Joseph DiGiorgio acquired California's attitudes toward farm labor, and the power to make them stick. Through interlocking directorates, his company was linked to the state's major financial, industrial, real estate, and retail institutions. Backed by the full weight of California's economic hierarchy, DiGiorgio broke every farm labor strike against it. In 1939, over 600 workers walked out of the company's Marysville orchards demanding a wage increase of from twenty-five to thirty cents an hour. After ten days of picketing, the company gave in, but two months later laid off some Anglo workers and replaced them with Filipino and Japanese crews. Again the workers struck. But under a new Yuba County anti-picketing ordinance, some 200 were arrested. Other strikers, according to a report made by U. S. Senator Robert LaFollette, were beaten up, put in a car, and driven out of the county without benefit of arrest or trial. When some of these deportees returned with union funds to set up a soup kitchen, it was raided and sacked by a sheriff's posse. The law had little sympathy for the strikers. At the arraignment of some sixty picketers, three of whom had been badly mauled by sheriff's deputies, a local judge told them: "You fellows can either plead guilty to vagrancy and the anti-picketing ordinance and I will give you six months in jail with a suspended sentence out of the county, or you can plead not guilty and demand a lawyer and we will give you a six man jury, and they will find you guilty and I will give you six months in jail, and you can do it in jail. What do you want to do, plead guilty or not guilty?

In 1947 and again in 1960, there were other strikes

against DiGiorgio ranches. As usual, there was violence—the 1947 strike culminated in the shooting of a National Farm Labor Union official by an unknown gunman—and as usual DiGiorgio was able to hold out against the strikers. Today the president of the company is Robert DiGiorgio, a nephew of the founder. For nearly a week, I tried to arrange an appointment with him at the company offices in San Francisco; he finally sent word through a public-relations man that he would not see me. The company's position, however, was clearly laid out in a blizzard of press releases given me by the PR man. "DiGiorgio is not opposed to unionization under conditions which assure the rights of both parties," one release said. "Our analysis of the current Delano disturbance, however, has convinced us that those who have requested meetings with us do not represent our employees. Our employees have so informed us."

The Delano growers stood on the assumption that they knew more about their workers than Cesar Chavez did. How much they knew is a moot point, as evidenced in an interview Robert DiGiorgio gave to the SNCC newspaper, *The Movement*. "I would like you to believe that the Di-Giorgio Corporation is as concerned for the welfare and dignity of our workers as anyone," he said. "Of course, since our Sierra Vista ranch near Delano is up for sale, the facilities there are not up to the standard of our other ranches. We simply cannot justify capital investment on property that is to be sold. There is a further problem the grower faces. If a steelworker takes his pay out and drinks it up and doesn't provide for his wife and family and lives in a hovel, then no one blames U. S. Steel. But if a farm worker does the same thing, it's the grower's fault. We can't be our brother's keeper. We can't be responsible for the manner in which our employees spend their money and their time."

DiGiorgio was the one grower able to get under Chavez's skin. "They're animals," Chavez said to me one day. "You can't trust them. The other growers tell you something and you can be fairly sure they'll do it. Not DiGiorgio." With Schenley out of the picture, Chavez focused the boycott on DiGiorgio's S&W and TreeSweet canned food and fruit products. So pejorative were the DiGiorgio brand names to the strikers that at the NFWA warehouse in Delano, strikers refused to take S&W canned goods which had been donated to the strike fund. "I had to tell them it wasn't poison," Chavez told me with a smile. "I told them, 'You can eat it, just don't buy it.'"

Inundated by unfavorable publicity, DiGiorgio sought a way to neutralize Chavez. Early in April, DiGiorgio indicated its willingness to let workers at its Sierra Vista ranch in Delano vote on the question of union representation. Chavez immediately countered with the demand that DiGiorgio, like Schenley, unilaterally recognize the NFWA. DiGiorgio refused, but for the first time the door was opened for negotiations. For the next two months, amid charge and countercharge of bad faith, the union and the company haggled. Twice, talks broke down, the first time after a scuffle outside Sierra Vista when, according to sworn testimony, a DiGiorgio security guard clubbed an NFWA woman picket over the head. Late in May, DiGiorgio won a temporary injunction against NFWA picketing at Sierra Vista. When the matter was finally heard before the Tulare County Superior Court, the injunction was denied. "No acts of violence were shown to have been committed by defendants [the NFWA] or their agents," Judge Leonard M. Ginzburg wrote in his decision. "Numerous acts of violence were shown by undisputed evidence to have been committed by plaintiff DiGiorgio agents."

It was at this juncture that the already virulent, already complex strike situation was even further entangled by the appearance on the Delano scene of the Teamsters' Union. Up to this moment, the Teamsters, especially locals in San Francisco and in Southern California, had been among Chavez's most vociferous supporters. The Southern California Teamsters had passed a resolution supporting the NFWA, and it was the San Francisco Teamsters, by their refusal to cross NFWA picket lines, who had helped break Schenley's back. Now the Teamsters announced that in fact they were candidates at DiGiorgio's Sierra Vista election, and, to Chavez's chagrin, they moved into Delano to battle the NFWA for the right to organize Sierra Vista.

Just why the Teamsters chose this moment to cut Chavez's legs out from under him is a study in labyrinthine union politics. Teamster president Jimmy Hoffa had little interest in the farm workers. "I was asked to draw up a budget for a farm organizing drive," one Teamster official recalls, "and when Hoffa saw it, he did a triple back flip and somersault." Along with the enormous cost and the multifarious organizing problems, there was the fact that Hoffa simply did not want to get involved at a time when he was fighting to stay out of jail for allegedly tampering with a jury in Memphis, Tennessee. "With all the troubles he's got," a Teamster official told me, "Hoffa needs the farm workers like he needs a hole in the head."

But the director of the Western Conference of Teamsters, Einar O. Mohn, had long been an enemy of Hoffa's in the union hierarchy. According to Teamsters friendly to Hoffa, Mohn thought that if he could organize the farm workers, he would be one of the rulers of the union in the event that Hoffa did go to prison. And with Hoffa beleaguered by the courts, Mohn knew the Teamster president would make no move to stop him.

The Mohn camp, however, insists that the decision to go into Delano was not a devious power play, but simply a bread-and-butter decision. The Teamsters have often found their economic interests intertwined like grape vines with those of the growers, most notably when the Teamsters, alone in union circles, favored the retention of the *bracero* program. In California, the Teamsters represent 100,000 workers directly dependent on agriculture, ranging from cannery and packing-shed workers to truck drivers who haul crops and process food. The prospect of a potentially unfriendly union representing farm workers was intolerable to Mohn, because if the NFWA called a strike, Teamster cannery and packing-shed workers, as well as Teamster truck drivers, would be thrown out of work.

Whatever the reasons, Delano welcomed the Teamsters. Growers who not long before had regarded Hoffa as the devil incarnate now saw him as the Redeemer. After months of siege, Delano had reluctantly begun to accept the inevitability of a union and saw in the Teamsters a way finally to take revenge on Chavez. "If the only way we can get that son of a bitch is by falling in bed with Hoffa, then we'll fall in bed with Hoffa," one grower told me. "It was almost embarrassing," a Teamster official said. "It was like the town was being shot up for eight months by a gunslinger and was just waiting for someone to come along and save it. They knew that we were gunslingers too. But they put a badge on us anyway, hoping that when we'd meet up with Chavez, we'd bump each other off."

DiGiorgio made no secret of its preference for the Teamsters. In the office of Sierra Vista's personnel manager, there was a hand-lettered placard reading: "NFWA —No Fair Working Association—They'd Rather Agitate Than Work." One DiGiorgio forewoman, who was known to support the NFWA and who had been with the company twenty-four years (even though she was only thirty-eight years old), was fired on the pretext that her work had "deteriorated," even though two days before her dismissal she had been assigned to teach inexperienced girls how to tip grape bunches. Though the NFWA could not venture onto company property without fear of arrest (the citizen's arrest had become a minor art form in Delano), the Teamsters, with company connivance if not official sanction, used DiGiorgio foremen and supervisory personnel to proselytize field and shed workers. Several foreladies threatened their crews with firing if they did not sign with the Teamsters. Another crew, according to sworn testimony, was told "there were two unions, one of them rich and one of them poor. The union of Mr. Chavez was very poor. It had to ask other unions for loans. It would benefit us to go where there was more money, to the Teamsters' Union, which even lent money to banks and foreign countries."

In San Francisco, meanwhile, DiGiorgio and the NFWA were still hammering out ground rules for the election. Chavez had even agreed to discuss a no-harvest-strike clause for the duration of any contract. On June 20, Chavez met with DiGiorgio officials and suggested that the NFWA, like the Teamsters, be given free access to campaign on DiGiorgio property and that the company and the union issue a joint statement announcing the election.

What happened next is an open question. DiGiorgio maintains that the "date of the election was communicated to Mr. Chavez, as were election rules, eligibility, and campaign procedures." Chavez, however, says that when he left DiGiorgio's San Francisco headquarters that afternoon, it had only been agreed that the election would be held "at a future date." Thirty-six hours later, DiGiorgio called a press conference and unilaterally announced that the election would be held at Sierra Vista two days hence. But word of the press conference leaked to the NFWA and it was invaded by William Kircher, the AFL-CIO's director of organizing, and Dolores Huerta, an NFWA vice president. They clashed angrily with Robert DiGiorgio and called the proposed election a "phony," declaring, in Mrs. Huerta's words, that it was organized in "bad faith," since the NFWA had, "as late as last night, been negotiating the conditions under which an election might be held."

Chavez was furious. From a contact in the Printers' Union, he learned that DiGiorgio had had the ballots printed before his last meeting with the company. "All the time we were sitting there, they knew they were going to pull a fast one," he told me. "How can you trust people like that?" The following day, the NFWA went into court and got a restraining order removing its name from the ballot. Charging DiGiorgio with dishonesty and bad faith, the NFWA announced that it would boycott the election.

The June 24 vote was, depending on whom one talked to in Delano, either the "phony election" or the "exercise in democracy." Both sides resorted to the most blatant kind of intimidation. The NFWA set up a picket line outside the polling place at Sierra Vista, and when the truckloads of workers rolled up to vote, they set up a din, shouting "Don't vote, don't vote, *huelga, huelga.*" One priest snapped pictures of the voters as they climbed off the trucks, warning them that the NFWA would know if they voted. The opposition was equally guilty. Two Anglo women hung a "Teamsters Forever" sign outside the polling place. When one truckload of workers asked what would happen if they did not vote, an interpreter told them they would be fired. Many workers who did not vote were trucked back to the polling place and warned to vote or else. One woman who was brought back a second time testified that a girl entered the polling booth with her and told her to vote for the Teamsters. Frightened, she did.

The vote count resulted in victory claims by both sides. Of the 385 workers casting ballots, 284 said they wanted to be represented by a union, and 281 of these specified the Teamsters. But Chavez pointed out that 347 workers —nearly half of the 732 eligible—heeded his boycott call and did not vote, making this, in his words, an "astounding victory." He further announced that picketing and the economic boycott would continue. And so Delano girded for a long hot summer.

THIRTEEN

The Sierra Vista vote brought relations between Chavez and DiGiorgio to their most abrasive point. Four days after the election, Chavez went to Borrego Springs, near San Diego, to try to pull workers out of DiGiorgio's ranch there. Through the day, he managed to persuade ten workers to walk out. DiGiorgio was willing to let the workers back on company property to pick up their checks and belongings, but refused to let an NFWA representative accompany them. The workers, however, claimed they were afraid of being harassed by the company's security guards and police dogs. With Wayne Hartmire of the Migrant Ministry and Father Victor Salandini, a Catholic priest, Chavez decided to court arrest by trespassing on company property with the workers. "He was, of course," Reverend Hartmire later noted in a memo, "not overlooking the strategic importance of such a confrontation."

The men had no sooner ventured into the camp than a DiGiorgio guard placed all thirteen under the ubiquitous citizen's arrest for trespassing on company property after work hours. The incident might quietly have ended there had the San Diego County sheriff's office not appeared on the scene to transport the thirteen to jail. With the exception of Father Salandini, the men were all stripped naked and chained together by the deputies. Once again, the NFWA benefited from the overkill instinct of its opponents, for when the episode was reported in the press, Chavez's clear legal guilt was obscured by the humiliating stripping and chaining of Reverend Hartmire, Chavez himself, and the ten workers.

The situation had clearly deteriorated to a point where Governor Pat Brown, despite his reluctance to get involved, could no longer remain aloof. Brown was in deep political trouble, his chances for reelection to a third term in November diminishing by the minute. In the Democratic primary held earlier in the month, he had been able to eke out only a narrow victory over Sam Yorty, the mayor of Los Angeles, while in the Republican primary, Ronald Reagan had steamrollered his opposition. Needing every vote he could muster, Brown was now warned by the Mexican-American Political Association, whose endorsement of statewide Democratic candidates had in the past been more or less *pro forma*, that he could not count on its support unless the DiGiorgio election was investigated. Yielding to MAPA's pressure, Brown, on June 28, the day before the Borrego Springs incident, appointed Dr. Ronald Haughton of Detroit's Wayne State University and the American Arbitration Association to look into the DiGiorgio voting.

Sixteen days later, after talking to all the principals in the dispute, Haughton recommended that a new election be held, at the same time emphasizing that his recommendation was neither "a condemnation nor an endorsement" of the previous vote. DiGiorgio and the Teamsters immediately accepted the proposal and the NFWA agreed to vote on it. The NFWA meeting was held at the Filipino Hall on the West Side. It is a one-story white stucco building with tattered and faded green facing. In the midsummer heat of the hall itself, crepe paper and tinsel Christmas decorations still hung from the aluminum ceiling lights. On the left wall, there were tinted photographs of past presidents of the Filipino Women's Club; on the right, a crude cartoon of Jesus Christ carrying the cross, with a grower exhorting scabs to jump on it to make His load heavier.

There was standing room only at the meeting. Extra benches had to be brought in from the outside to accommodate the overflow. Little children played in the aisles, undisciplined by their parents, many of whom were fanning themselves with the Filipino newspaper *Laging Una,* which, among other things, in a front-page editorial denounced Lyndon Johnson as a "madman" and "megalomaniac" whose "fanatical expression," "cracked voice," and "feeble croak" were "startlingly reminscent of the Fuehrer as he defended the aggressions of German fascism and his own role as a god on earth." As usual, Chavez was late, and after an opening prayer by Father Salandini, the meeting was given over to NFWA business. The Reverend James Drake of the Migrant Ministry, displaying a rather fanciful notion of the economic process, attributed a drop in the price of DiGiorgio stock to the boycott. "It's the lowest it's ever been," he said happily. "It's down to 19¾." Portentously, he added: "But it doesn't seem to get any lower. They must be keeping it up artificially by buying it themselves."

Drake then announced that because of the NFWA's precarious finances, only the cars of the oldest *huelguistas* could be repaired at the camp. "Cars," he said, his voice rising, "that are falling apart because of DiGiorgio and the other growers." Finally, he cautioned that the NFWA's telephone bill the previous month had risen to $1,600 and that, accordingly, locks had been placed on the phones to stop profligate long-distance calling. Already the locks had been broken twice, he said, "and if we find out who did it, we'll take action."

After forty-five minutes of this, Chavez walked in. The cheering welled up and he seemed genuinely embarrassed. Very quietly, when the noise died down, he explained that if they accepted the Haughton recommendations, it meant that the NFWA would have to give up the boycott and picketing against DiGiorgio and that if the election were lost the NFWA could neither resume such activities nor seek another vote for one year. "We had to give up a lot to get this," he said. "I think it's a good thing."

The vote carried unanimously and Chavez threw the meeting open to questions. Someone asked what would happen to workers who, in the event that the NFWA won the election, still would not join the union. Chavez smiled and said that the same question had come up during negotiations over the Schenley contract, when the company told him that four workers refused to join the NFWA. "I told them," he said, " 'You did such a good job indoctrinating them *against* us, you should be able to do an equally good job indoctrinating them *for* us. If not, fire them.' "

The meeting adjourned with the singing of *Nosotros Venceremos,* which is *We Shall Overcome* in Spanish. In the crush at the front of the hall, I introduced myself to Father Salandini. He is tall and much younger-looking than his forty years, and never seems to be without a folder of press clippings detailing his skirmishes with Church superiors in the past decade. Over Chavez's name, he had written a letter on NFWA stationery to his bishop in San Diego, explaining the circumstances of his arrest in

Borrego Springs, and he was now trying to get Chavez to sign it. It was nearly midnight and he had a six-hour drive back to San Diego. "I'm supposed to say Mass at six-thirty," he told me. "I guess I'll call my pastor and tell him I had a flat tire."

The acceptance of the Haughton Report by all three parties, and the announcement of August 30 as the new election date, did not ease tensions in Delano. Four days after the NFWA approved the report, DiGiorgio suddenly laid off 190 workers at Sierra Vista. Over the telephone, Dick Myer, DiGiorgio's personnel manager, told me that the layoff was natural at that time of year; once the viniculture was completed, he said, there was always a two- or three-week layoff before picking began. Chavez, however, was convinced that the layoff was a ploy on the part of DiGiorgio to get rid of sure NFWA votes, and early that afternoon he drove out to Sierra Vista to try to persuade as many of the 190 as possible to remain in Delano until the election. (Under the terms of the agreement, anyone who had worked for DiGiorgio for fifteen days in the past year was eligible to vote in the election.)

The sun was blistering. The laid-off workers milled around seeking shade under the few isolated palm trees on the edge of the Sierra Vista property. Four Tulare County sheriff's cars had drawn up and the deputies idled about, surveying the scene. Just inside the Sierra Vista property line a young Anglo DiGiorgio employee with a movie camera was taking pictures of every move Chavez made. Weary and unshaven, Chavez climbed up on the roof of an old station wagon, and as he did, the DiGiorgio photographer moved into better camera position. Motioning to an NFWA volunteer with a camera, Chavez said angrily, "Take some pictures of that guy taking pictures of me."

Waving a bullhorn, Chavez asked for quiet. He told the workers that the NFWA wanted them to remain in Delano. Their votes were necessary, he said, if there was ever to be a farm union, and he told them that the NFWA would provide them with room and board and try to get them work. Chavez looked glum. He knew he could never find enough work for the 190, and once they had scattered, it was unlikely that they would return to Delano to vote. I was standing at the edge of the crowd beside a boy in his late teens wearing an army fatigue jacket with his name, Lopez, stitched over the pocket. Myer had told me that the work in the fields was all finished and I asked Lopez if this were so. "We didn't even finish what we started this morning," he said. "There's some rows half finished. They just brought us back for lunch and told us we'd be paid off at five o'clock." ("The workers to be laid off were given the usual term of notice," DiGiorgio's attorney later wrote me. "When the bulk of the work is substantially complete, it is normal practice to pay off the crews; supervisors and crew managers complete the rows.")

Across the road, some of the workers, mainly women wearing tattered mantillas, began kneeling in the dust behind a battered Mercury station wagon decked with flowers and covered with crepe paper and brick-patterned wallpaper. This was the NFWA strike vigil, kept around the clock there across from the Sierra Vista railroad siding. *Huelga* posters and American and Mexican flags adorned the car; the tailgate was open and in the back of the station wagon was a portrait of the Virgin of Guadalupe, surrounded by blankets and bedrolls for the workers who maintained the vigil at night. When Chavez finished speaking, the pickers slowly dispersed and the women in dust started to chant the rosary.

That night, Chavez called a strike meeting at Lake Woollomes, a bleak dusty park off the Friant-Kern irrigation canal on the outskirts of Delano. The heat had broken and a radio was playing Mexican music and the workers sat around drinking soda and chatting among themselves. Chavez sat at a barbecue table filling out forms for some of the laid-off workers who had come from Texas and now claimed that DiGiorgio would not pay their fare home. The only thing that buoyed him was the presence of some Sierra Vista workers who had previously refused to recognize either the strike or the NFWA, but who now, because of the layoff of the 190, were signing NFWA authorization cards. One of the volunteers asked Chavez if he wanted anything and he smiled wearily. "Just get me some canned sleep," he said. "Eight hours concentrated."

Later that evening, I drove Chavez home. It had been a long and hectic day and he was almost corroded with fatigue. The layoff had been a blow, not only because of the votes lost but because it had cost him some twenty organizers he had infiltrated into the DiGiorgio camp. "That's why they did this," he said bitterly, "to get rid of those guys. We've pulled four sets of people out of there and every time we've had to start all over again."

I asked if he had anyone left inside Sierra Vista.

"They left five women in the women's camp, all against us," he said. "They left all the old Filipinos, the ones who are pensioned. Normally they're the first to go, but they're still there, and the Filipinos don't like Mexicans. They left all the Japanese, and of all the racial groups, the Japs are the most violently against us." He told me that a week or two before, when he was permitted to go into Sierra Vista with Haughton, the Japanese cook in one camp loudly banged his pots and pans whenever they tried to speak.

Most of Chavez's bitterness, however, was reserved for the Teamsters. "Those bastards," he said. "We shook the tree and now they're trying to pick up the fruit. That's how they operate. And if they get away with it this time, we'll never get them off our back. Just when we get a grower softened up, they'll come in and try to make a deal with him. That's the way they do it, through the bosses."

Almost pensively, he said that he really wasn't surprised that DiGiorgio so openly favored the Teamsters. "After all," he said, with a certain amount of pride, "we pushed them into this position. They know we're a social union. And this is their way of getting us."

I asked how he thought the election would turn out.

"It's tough enough just fighting a company," he said. "Or it's tough enough just fighting another union. But when the company and the union are working hand in glove, it's a hard combination to beat."

FOURTEEN

In early August 1966, I decided to leave the Valley and come back for the election, still a month off. I flew to Honolulu for ten days, glad to get away for a while from the heat, the bitterness, and the self-righteousness rampant on both sides of the freeway in Delano. While I was in Honolulu, I talked to representatives of the International Longshoremen's and Warehousemen's Union, which after several notoriously acrimonious years in the late forties had managed to organize Hawaii's farm labor force. With the passage of time, tempers have cooled, and Jack Hall, the ILWU leader who was once convicted under the Smith Act for conspiring to teach the overthrow of the United States government by force, has become a member of Hawaii's establishment, praised by the press for his civic activities, commended by the Island oligarchy for being "tough but fair," and in turn dispenser of bromides to the women of the Outdoor Circle for their efforts in "preserving the loveliness that is Hawaii." I could not help but wonder if such a fate would be Cesar Chavez's, or if time would benefit Valley farm workers as it has those in Hawaii. Mechanization has trimmed the work force in Island sugar from 35,000 in 1945 to 10,500 now. The average hourly earnings, including fringe benefits, are now in excess of $3. The laborers work a forty-hour week, with overtime thereafter, and have comprehensive medical plans, pensions, paid vacations and holidays, sick leave, severance pay, and, for those who cannot get work during the off season, unemployment insurance. It seemed a long way from the Valley.

When I returned to Delano, a few days before the election, it was as if I had not left. In the weeks before the election, Chavez, in need of money and organizing strength for his battle with the Teamsters, had merged the NFWA with AWOC and taken his union into the AFL-CIO. The name of the merged union was the United Farm Workers Organizing Committee. Negotiations between AWOC and the NFWA had been going on since the start of the strike, despite the opposition of Al Green, the old-line labor organizer and head of AWOC, who distrusted both Chavez and his supporters in the New Left. Unofficially, however, Larry Itliong, AWOC's chief organizer in Delano, continued to cooperate with Chavez with the tacit support of William Kircher, the AFL-CIO's national director of organizing. "Kircher told me not to worry about Al Green," Itliong said to me one day. "He said he'd take care of him. So I began bypassing Green and working directly with Kircher. Finally, in August, Cesar and Kircher and I decided, 'Let's do it.'" There were numerous advantages to the merger. With two unions, both money and personnel were divided, and there was also a potentially uncomfortable racial situation between the Mexicans and the Filipinos, who had little love for each other. A united front not only would permit both unions to receive AFL-CIO support, but it was also thought that a close working association would relieve whatever strain existed between the Mexicans and the Filipinos. Both unions agreed to the merger, although there was some grumbling from the Filipinos in AWOC, who feared that the Mexican-Americans would have the major voice in union affairs. In protest, two top AWOC organizers in Delano quit the union and were immediately snapped up by the Teamsters. "One guy told me the union didn't belong to the Filipinos any more," Chavez told me. "That's because I had taken it over."

Nor were the volunteers pleased by the merger. My first night back in Delano, I encountered a number of them in the bar at People's and, to my surprise, they seemed to regard the merger as Chavez's Munich. One told me that Chavez had "sold out" the farm workers to the AFL-CIO, which, like all institutions, was "corrupt." Another, more temperate, thought Chavez should have waited until the NFWA was "strong enough to change the AFL-CIO from the inside. He could have been a moral force, like Malcolm X with the Negroes." I suggested that Chavez's first obligation to his members was to win the election, and that without the resources of the AFL-CIO, it was extremely unlikely that he could. "Maybe you're right," the volunteer reluctantly concurred. "But the romance is gone." I asked Chavez how he had dealt with the volunteer situation. "I told them that the grass roots had to run the strike," he said. "I said they were here as servants of the union, not to run the show, and that they had to work disinterested in the politics of the union."

The morning after my return, I visited the AFL-CIO headquarters, which was set up in the back of a barbershop on the West Side. There were unmade cots all over the office, and a mimeograph machine was grinding out leaflets to be distributed to the workers in the fields. On a table were stacks of copies of Senator Robert Kennedy's indictment of the Teamsters, *The Enemy Within*, extracts of which had been printed in both English and Spanish. I leafed through some of the pamphlets. "Have the Teamsters told you the Teamster pension fund is UNDER A FEDERAL PROBE?" asked one. Another, lifted from *The Enemy Within*, quoted Jimmy Hoffa threatening the general counsel of the AFL-CIO Retail Clerks Union: "Don't you know I could have you killed? I've got friends who would shoot you in your tracks one day while you were just walking down the street. If I did it, no jury would ever convict me. I have a special way with juries."

The head of the Delano operation was William Kircher, the tall, quiet-spoken man who is the AFL-CIO's director of organizing. I asked him what effect the leaflets were having. "If we win this election," he said, tapping a copy of *The Enemy Within*, "this will be what did it. That Kennedy name is magic." He asked if I had read an article in the latest issue of *Life* which had been generally favorable to Hoffa. I said I had. "Everyone knows that Jimmy Hoffa is the biggest Republican in the labor movement," Kircher said. "And there's no doubt that Henry Luce is a Republican. Now you can't tell me there's not some kind of collusion."

I did not try to.

Later that morning I stopped in at Teamster headquarters in Room 208 of the Stardust Motel. Outside the office was a row of cars, all new models, including a Cadillac and a Thunderbird, plastered with blue and silver posters which said simply "TEAMSTERS." A half dozen Teamster organizers lounged around outside, drinking beer and comparing golf scores. Some had changed into swimming trunks and were trying to get the others to take a dip in the Stardust pool before lunch. Sitting inside the office was a pinched and lacquered blond secretary reading a copy of *The Enemy Within*.

The quiet confidence of Room 208 was most marked in the person of William Grami, who ramrodded the Teamster organizing force in Delano. What seemed to perturb Grami most about the NFWA was its lack of Teamster professionalism. "They're not even a union," he told me. "They're a civil-rights organization. The AFL-CIO made a big mistake. If it had been me, instead of merging with Chavez, I would have kept him on a leash, used him to scare hell out of the growers, and then gone in and picked up the pieces."

I pointed out that this seemed to be what the Teamsters were doing, and he shrugged. I asked what he thought of the NFWA's agreement with Schenley and how it compared with any contract that the Teamsters might get. "All they've got is a memorandum of agreement," he said softly. "If that's a contract, then I'm a Mexican."

The main thrust of the Teamster campaign was to Red-bait the NFWA in much the same way that the AFL-CIO was gangster-baiting the Teamsters. Copies of an article in the John Birch Society magazine labeling the whole Delano strike as Communist-inspired had been translated into Spanish and passed out in the fields. One Teamster pamphlet said that a vote for the Teamsters was a vote "against revolution, hatred of one race against another, the New Left, riots, beatniks, and destruction of the field crops that feed the nation." Grami himself, choosing his words fastidiously, always referred to the NFWA as the "Vietcong."

"We told the Vietcong that if they persisted in calling us

gangsters, we'd fight fire with fire," he said. "They say we use Birch Society tactics. Well, they've got seniority on us in that issue. It's personally distasteful to me, but if the shoe fits, wear it. And the merger with the AFL-CIO doesn't make them any more respectable. You'll notice they haven't got rid of any of the New Left crowd."

Grami would not consider the prospect of losing the election, but finally admitted that even a Teamster loss would not cause any undue trouble. "If we lose, we'll organize faster," he said. "If Chavez wins, he becomes that much more potent. And the growers are already afraid of him, scared of the lengths to which he'll go. So they'll come to us that much quicker."

I asked Grami about reports that Teamster organizers had roughed up several NFWA members a few days before. He smiled slowly. "We've been right here at the Stardust," he said. "No one's brought any charges against us. This is a tough town, things happen here. Why, there's been six murders just since I've been here. And not one of those so-called beatings was serious, you'll notice. A belt in the nose here, a punch in the eye there."

As we talked, a Teamster organizer came into the office. "Bill, did you hear about that priest at the vigil this morning?" he asked. "Did you hear what he said about us? Why, I'd like to . . ."

"No, you wouldn't," Grami said soothingly. "The last thing we need is for somebody to take a poke at a priest."

That afternoon, I drove out to Sierra Vista for the last hours of campaigning. I stopped first at the vigil. A young man in blue denim work clothes whom I recognized as a volunteer was taking pictures. I introduced myself to him, but he jammed his hand into his pocket. "Are you a Teamster?" he asked through clenched teeth. "I don't have enough handshakes to pass any out to Teamsters." I shook my head and got back into the car. At all the camps, DiGiorgio had passed out a series of letters urging workers to vote for the Teamsters. "The Teamsters do not want support from beatniks, out-of-town agitators, or do-gooders," said one letter I found tacked on a camp bulletin board. Parked under a stand of trees a short distance away was a big Teamster bus stocked with beer and soda, which Teamster organizers were passing out to workers with a show of geniality. Two Teamster sound trucks cruised the camps, trying to shout down NFWA organizers.

"Hey, I'm going to tell your wife about that little girl," the driver of one Teamster van blared over his loudspeaker at an AFL-CIO organizer. "How old is she? Eighteen? Man, that alimony will kill you."

"That's okay, man," the organizer shouted back. "At least I've got my manhood. That's more than you can still say. You're all run down."

"You'd like to be run down like me, man," the Teamster laughed.

"Not on your life, man. I hear they got you for molesting a little girl. Nine years old is what I hear."

"You're a comedian, man," the Teamster said. "Jackie Gleason ought to sign you up."

"You sound scared, man. You're going to lose tomorrow. What's Hoffa going to do about that? Hoffa don't like losers."

I tailed one of the Teamster vans into a clearing where some hundred workers were sitting under the trees trying to escape the heat. The driver of the truck was a Teamster named Art Chavarria. He was a big man with a pencil mustache, a mountain of black hair piled on top of his head, a raucous laugh, and a capacity for nonstop talking without losing his temper. He spotted a woman talking to an NFWA organizer and drove his truck over to where they stood. "Honey," Chavarria said over his mike, "what do you want to talk to the Vietcong for? You want to learn about Cuba, you want to learn about the Commies, you talk to Valdez. He's very big with Castro, I hear. Yeah, I hear he's Castro's adviser to Chavez. That's right from the horse's mouth. Sure, that's why he spent so much time in Cuba. You mean you didn't *know?* They're keeping that a *secret?* Honey, you come over here and I'll tell you all about it."

Chavarria was clearly enjoying himself and looked around for another target. At the edge of the group gathered around his truck was a young Anglo girl wearing baggy pants and a dirty blue sweater. "Now don't tell me," Chavarria said. "I bet I can guess. I bet you're for Chavez. See, she's blushing. I'm right. Honey, you look like a college girl. I can always tell a college girl. The class always shows." A burst of phlegmy laughter escaped over the microphone. "Tell me, what college you go to? Really, I want to know. I got five kids and I don't want to send them to that college."

"Why don't you go home, you bum?" shouted a woman field worker wearing red slacks.

"These people always dress the part," Chavarria laughed. "What color are your pants, lady?"

A bearded NFWA photographer stepped to the door of Chavarria's truck and began snapping his picture. "I'm easygoing, baby," Chavarria said, "but I just hope you try to take a picture of me the day after tomorrow."

"That's right, Art, you just keep talking," the photographer said. "You make a good picture."

"We're going to win tomorrow," Chavarria said. "And we're going to celebrate. That's the nice part of being with the Teamsters. We're not going to cuss you. We're going to say, 'Good morning, ladies. Good morning, gents.'"

"You just go on believing that, Art," the photographer said.

"I notice you're the only one here with a Japanese camera," Chavarria said. "You're not even a good American."

"You said it, Art."

Chavarria looked at the photographer's beard. "Hey, baby, I was a barber once. You need a shave, I'll give it to you." Then he elaborately took his nose between his fingers. "Baby, I don't mind you taking my picture," he said. "But you smell. You take my picture, you stand downwind. I'll tell you what. You stand downwind and I'll get you some of that stuff you squeeze under your arm. It's good. It gives one-day protection."

The presence of the photographer was beginning to irritate two other Teamster organizers who were standing at the back of the group.

"Why don't you bust him in the chops with that mike, Chavarria," said one.

"That's right," said the other. "Jam it right in his mush."

That night, the Teamster organizers gathered in the bar of the Stardust Motel. They were quiet and smelled of shaving lotion and were so confident that they did not discuss the election at all. They reminded me of a superbly conditioned professional football team on the eve of a match with a pickup squad of local all-stars. A short distance away, in the Filipino Hall, the NFWA was holding an election rally. The auditorium was jammed and reeked of sweat and cigarette smoke and excitement. Hoots of laughter shook the hall as El Teatro Campesino performed a skit about collusion between DiGiorgio and the Teamsters.

"What's the AFL-CIO, boss?" an actor playing a picker asked another, who was wearing a large white card identifying him as "DiGiorgio."

"It's a bunch of Communists," the boss answered.

The feature of the evening was a pair of films lent by the United Auto Workers showing the plight of migratory workers during the Depression. Shot after shot of farm labor camps flickered across the screen. Wan women nursed dirty, emaciated children; defeated men shoveled gruel on to their plates from a community pot and sat smoking listlessly in front of their grubby pup tents. Intercut in the film were shots of happy, well-fed celebrants at the 1933 Chicago World's Fair "Century of Progress." Time and again, the camera cut away from a hobo jungle and hovered on a Fair billboard that said: "There's no way like the American way."

At last Chavez was called to speak. He stood uneasily in front of the audience, hands in his pockets, a trace of a smile on his face, waiting for the applause to die down. "I think we have done all the work that is necessary," he said. "I hope that with the help of God we will be victorious. Thank you."

The voting began at seven o'clock the next morning at Sierra Vista. The polling booths were covered with red, white and blue curtains. Some 1,800 workers were eligible, 700 of whom were actually at work at DiGiorgio that day; the balance were eligible because they had worked at Sierra Vista at some point during the year. These were the unknown quantity who, if they appeared in Delano to cast their ballots, could swing the outcome. There were, in fact, to be two elections, one for the shed workers and the other, by far the larger and more significant for both the Teamsters and the NFWA, for the pickers.

The press was in a roped-off enclave a hundred feet from the polling place. A young CBS correspondent wearing an immaculate white linen jacket stood in front of a television camera making his prognostication. "After four days here," he confided into his microphone, "all signs point to a Teamster victory. This is Terry Drinkwater, speaking from Delano." Two women, one wearing tennis shoes, stood in the press section snapping pictures of every reporter and photographer who passed through. I saw them talking to an officer of Citizens for Facts and later one of them asked me the name of the bearded NFWA photographer. I in turn asked her name.

"Mary Smith," she said, turning away.

"And your friend?"

"Mary Brown," she tossed back over her shoulder.

A tall rumpled man entered the press section and was immediately surrounded by reporters. His name was Donald Connors and he was a member of the San Francisco law firm which represented DiGiorgio. For the first time, DiGiorgio seemed to be losing its composure about the results of the election. The NFWA, he said, had violated the Haughton agreement so often that DiGiorgio had ample grounds to challenge if Chavez won. He was asked if there had been any Teamster violations.

"I haven't heard of any," he said.

"Will you challenge if Chavez wins?"

"I'm a slow thinker," Connors said. "I'll have to think that one over." He turned to Harry Bernstein, the able reporter for the Los Angeles *Times* whose coverage of the Delano situation had been perhaps the most thorough and balanced in the nation. "You haven't done a very good job reporting this story, Harry," he said fretfully.

Later that morning, I drove over to Teamster headquarters. The office was empty except for a secretary filing her nails with an emery board. The NFWA headquarters, however, was alive with activity. Scores of cars clogged the street outside the office and dozens of workers milled around on the sun-parched lawn. The NFWA had told all workers not in the fields to report to the office before going out to Sierra Vista so that the union could get a line on the number of votes it had. Each voter was checked off on a list and assigned to a car to take him out to the polling place. Tacked to the door of the office was a telegram: "Offering Mass for you and the success of the election on Tuesday. Monsignor Gerald Cox."

It was evident that the NFWA thought it could not rely wholly on the workers already in the fields at Sierra Vista for victory, but had to bring in as many eligibles as possible from outside Delano. On the wall inside the office were street maps of all the outlying towns, and cars were constantly dispatched to Wasco and Earlimart and Porterville and Pixley to pick up eligible voters. Other workers eligible to vote had answered the NFWA's mailed pleas for help and trekked into town from out of state. One man paid his own way up from Jalisco, Mexico, 2,000 miles away, and another had driven all the way from Mexico only to find that he was not eligible. A family of four who had come over from Texas had their car break down before they reached Delano. The father called NFWA headquarters to say they could not make it before the polls closed. "If you lose by four votes," he said, "I'll never forgive myself."

Late that evening, under police escort, officials of the American Arbitration Association, which had supervised the election, took the ballot boxes up to San Francisco for counting. The next afternoon, the final tally was announced. The Teamsters won the shed workers' vote, as expected, by a count of 94 to 43, with seven ballots for no union. But in the all-important field worker's election, the NFWA snowed the Teamsters under by a vote of 530 to 331, with twelve votes for no union. According to the AAA figures, 513 votes were cast by workers not currently employed at Sierra Vista, most of which went to the NFWA. Chavez's out-of-town policy had paid off.

The NFWA's victory rally at Filipino Hall was tumultuous. Priests, ministers, AFL-CIO organizers, students, workers, and weeping girls engulfed Chavez, throwing their arms around his neck, pulling him to and fro. A Mexican woman pushed her way to the stage and presented him with a painting of a monument erected in Mexico in

memory of the Revolution of 1910. Another woman field
worker, her dark face lit with emotion, handed him a
statue of Christ dressed in green and white robes. Slowly
Chavez raised the statue above his head.

"*Viva,*" they shouted.

"*Viva la huelga!*"

"*Viva la causa!*"

"*Viva Cesar Chavez!*"

FIFTEEN

It was not the beginning of the end; it was not even the end of the beginning. "This victory makes it a little easier, that's all," Chavez said after the vote was in. "We still have thirty growers to go." Nor was it easy to work out a contract between UFWOC and DiGiorgio. It took seven months and the services of a professional mediator before a mutually acceptable pact was agreed upon. The contract provided for a union shop, a minimum wage of $1.65 an hour, a guarantee of four hours "reporting and standby" pay if no work is available, and a week's paid vacation for workers employed 1,600 hours a year. The wage minimum is raised to $1.70 in 1968 and workers who have been with the company for three years will get two weeks' vacation.

The rest of Delano, however, remains defiant. In a single three-hour period one evening early in January, 1967, five fires were set in various offices maintained by the farm workers all over Delano. No suspects were uncovered. And for their part, the growers do not regard the Sierra Vista vote as an indication of things to come. I asked Jack Pandol one afternoon if the DiGiorgio results had not laid to rest the theory that farm workers do not want a union. His answer was echoed all over Delano's East Side. "The vote wasn't a normal pattern," he said. "These people don't vote. That's not their nature. Someone had to pay them to come here. We've heard the AFL-CIO spent $50,000 to bring in people from outside Delano to vote." I reminded him that of the 1,300 workers who had voted at Sierra Vista—some 300 ballots were challenged and not counted in the final tally—only nineteen had expressed a desire for no union at all. He would not budge. "It's not a normal pattern," he repeated.

And so with the deadening tenacity of the Hundred Years' War, the strike continues. Though the AFL-CIO has allotted $10,000 a month to UFWOC, the cost of maintaining the strikers has mounted to $40,000 a month. Food and clothing is still trucked into Delano every week, and every afternoon the wives of the strikers still line up outside the storehouse for their provisions. From Delano, the strike has spread into Starr County, Texas, where indigent Mexican pickers were being paid as little as forty cents an hour. The script is the same; only the locale is different. UFWOC's charges against Starr County growers and residents have a depressingly familiar ring—workers beaten by police, arrested without cause, fired without reason. The bitterness of the dispute brought an investigation by the U. S. Senate Subcommittee on Migratory Labor, which was so appalled by its findings that it turned them over to the Justice Department. His time in Delano already sliced thin, Chavez today must chop it even finer to give leadership and encouragement to the Texas strikers. In the summer of 1966, the NFWA staged a 400-mile march from the Rio Grande Valley to the state capital in Austin. The march dramatized the pickers' plight, but the crop was still picked, either by machines or by scab labor. Yet for the first time, the Mexican-American farm workers of Texas were striking out as an organized group, and the march, like the Delano march in California, held implications that could have a profound social and economic effect in south Texas.

Today throughout California and the Southwest, UFWOC claims 17,000 members. Moreover, the figures bely the growers' contention that they cannot afford unionization. In California, their dire predictions that the end of the *bracero* program meant economic disaster have proved false. Since the *bracero* law lapsed in December, 1964, California's agricultural income has increased from $3.7 billion to $4.08 billion, and the per farm net income has increased 14 percent over the 1960-64 average. A powerful chain of California newspapers is discussing backing Chavez for public office, and Senator Robert Kennedy has said that if it is possible to land a man on the moon by 1970, it would not seem impossible to improve the lot of farm workers. Yet after the initial successes with Schenley and DiGiorgio, the Delano grape strike bogged down. And the blame could be laid entirely to the hardly unexpected intransigence of the growers.

One reason was advanced by Saul Alinsky. "Let's face it," he told me one day. "The problem of the Mexican-Americans is an urban problem. There's one acid question you've got to ask yourself before you get involved in something like this: 'If we succeed, what have we got after we got it?' With the farm workers, you don't have much. It's like fighting on a constantly disintegrating bed of sand. The big problem is automation. In ten years, mechanization will make the historical farm worker obsolete. So what you've got to do is retrain the Mexican-Americans for urban living. Cesar doesn't understand this, any more than he understands that the majority of the AFL-CIO is middle class now. The thirties conditions simply don't exist any more. And on top of this, he doesn't like unions. He thinks they're all a bunch of rackets."

I asked Alinsky how he would have utilized his organizing talents had he been leading the strike. "First off, I would have got a patron," he said. "The farm workers aren't going to win this by themselves. When the SNCC kids and the civil-rights people leave, you're back on page 27 of the newspaper. The money tree stops and who cares. The small growers don't care about publicity. They can fight. That's when you need a patron, someone who can lean on the growers. I would have gone to Hoffa. I would have said, 'Listen, everyone thinks you're nothing but a goddam hoodlum. You need to pretty yourself up. And the way to do it is to help the poor migrant Mexican. You do it and people won't call you Hoodlum Hoffa any more. They'll be calling you *Huelga* Hoffa.'" Alinsky shook his head sadly. "Hoffa could have been the friend of the migrant Mexican. Jesus, he needed something. But now he's in the can."

Chavez was not unaware of either the benefits to be derived from a patron or the need for a detente with the Teamsters. A few weeks after the Sierra Vista vote, events began to bear out Grami's prediction that an NFWA victory would in the long run benefit the Teamsters because of grower antipathy to Chavez. Early in October, 1966, Fred Perelli-Minetti, one of the biggest independent growers in Delano, signed a contract with the Teamsters, giving them the right to bargain for his workers. Again the barrage of charge and countercharge hung over Delano. Chavez announced that he did not recognize the agreement and set up UFWOC pickets outside the Perelli-Minnetti vineyards.

Almost perfunctorily, the Teamsters fought back. But among Teamster leaders, a reassessment of the entire farm labor situation was taking place. Privately, they concluded that their union was being used by the growers to thwart Chavez's efforts. They also admitted the validity of Chavez's claim that traditional trade-union techniques were useless for organizing farm workers and that only by appealing to *la causa* could the grape pickers be unionized. Chavez was approached and early in January, 1967, a secret meeting was arranged at the Beverly Rodeo Hotel in Beverly Hills. Through the afternoon and evening, Chavez and the Teamsters worked out an agreement on almost every facet of farm labor organization. "The Teamsters were ready to sell Perelli-Minetti out that night," says an observer at the meeting. "They got in easy, they could have got out easy. Sidney Korshak was there and he could have tied up all the loose ends."

The agreement was sabotaged, however, by the longstanding antipathy of the AFL-CIO leadership toward the Teamsters. Moreover, the relationship between UFWOC and the AFL-CIO precluded Chavez from taking any action on his own. UFWOC is not an independent union affiliated with the AFL-CIO, but an organizing committee of the federation, and hence Chavez is subject, in a way that the leader of an independent affiliate is not, to the discipline and strictures of George Meany. Since the AFL-CIO ousted the Teamsters in 1957, there have been no direct relations between the two. Dozens of independent AFL-CIO affiliates, however, have mutual-aid agreements with the Teamsters. But Meany refuses to have anything to do with them. "He just hates Hoffa," says an official of the United Auto Workers. "It's a personality thing. He'll let anyone else play with the Teamsters. My God, he has to. We all have dealings with them every day. But he won't. And that means that anyone dependent on him for support —that takes in Cesar and UFWOC—can't play with them either."

For months, UFWOC treaded water. The momentum of the strike seemed to be slipping away. No headway was made against the growers and only the *pro forma* allegations of the Teamsters and UFWOC against each other ruffled the Valley as it eased back into the status quo. But backstage, an interfaith committee of California clergymen worked to resolve the differences between the two unions. Finally, in July 1967, the clergymen broke down the resistance of the AFL-CIO and an agreement was reached restoring peace between the Teamsters and Chavez. Under the terms of the agreement, UFWOC will have jurisdiction over all field workers, while the Teamsters will have jurisdiction over workers in canneries, creameries, frozen-food processing plants, dehydrating plants, and warehouses.

The settlement produced immediate results. On the day the agreement was announced, Gallo Winery, the largest in the world, Paul Masson and a number of other California wineries gave notice that they would hold union representation elections for all their field and processing workers. The bulk of California's growers, however, stood firm. In an angry statement, the Council of California Growers denounced the clergymen for their part in forming a "cartel designed to bludgeon California farmers until they respond to the whims of the powerful bosses of organized labor. It appears that these church leaders have now appointed themselves the ultimate authority as to who will decide what contracts are valid, who should be boycotted, who should be picketed and literally who does what to whom."

The agreement with the Teamsters at last gave Chavez the lever against the ranchers he had long sought. But it also posed a powerful dilemma. For two years, he had played a lone hand against the massed power of the Delano growers. Now, in effect, he has accepted a patron, and as a proud man, he is cognizant of the fact that he could become a figurehead in the movement that is his life. The technocrats are in a position to take over, men who have air-travel cards and speak the language of the bargaining table. The possibility first occurred to me at an NFWA rally one evening shortly before the DiGiorgio election. The workers spoke first, women with no teeth and men with dirt caked under their fingernails. They spoke haltingly of what the strike meant to them and their words held a lifetime of pride in the face of poverty. Then a young Anglo labor leader stood up. He was wearing a blue buttoned-down shirt and a blazer with gold buttons and he held out his hands and said, "Brothers and sisters." The incongruity first amused and then saddened me, for I wondered if the future of *la causa* lay in the hands of men who wore blazers with gold buttons.

It is a possibility of which Chavez is aware. "The danger is we will become like the building trades," he said once. "Our situation is similar, being the bargaining agents for many separate companies and contractors. We don't want to model ourselves on the industrial unions. That would be bad. We want to get involved in politics, in voter registration, not just contract negotiation. The trouble is that no institution can remain fluid. We have to find some cross between being a movement and being a union."

This is the dream every labor leader starts with. It is the movement, after all, not really the union, that is breaking up the whole social structure of the Valley. The growers are no longer firmly in control of a way of life they have run for a century, no longer the ultimate arbiters not only of their destiny but of the destiny of every man who works in the fields for them. Shortly before I left Delano, I talked to one of the growers. He was in a reflective mood. "God, we were stupid," he said. "All of us, right from the start. We should have banded together when this thing began, all the growers, and held an election right then. Chavez wouldn't have had a chance. No one had heard of him and that would have been the end of it. No publicity, no nothing. We would have been the good guys for holding the election and we would have won. And Chavez would have been finished." I asked why they had not done it. "Because we never had before," he said simply.

No man, no town likes to think it was wrong, and it was the bitterness of having been proven wrong that seemed to pervade Delano. The cherished assumption that the workers were happy and did not want a union had been exploded as fallacious. As the destroyer of the myth, Chavez was singled out for the most virulent hatred. And yet in a strange way, Delano has reaped an emotional profit from the strike. It is the biggest thing that has ever happened to the town. Talk though they do about the harm to Delano's image, the people there are caught up in a cause as they have never been caught up by anything else in their lives.

The effect of the strike on Delano reminds me of the last line of a poem by C. P. Cavafy in which the speaker, informed that the barbarians who have besieged the city's gates for decades are no longer there, murmurs with some regret: "And now what shall become of us without any barbarians? Those people were a kind of solution."

The question is what in the end will happen to "those people." The day I left Delano, I talked to William Kircher. "I told the workers they had to be prepared for the tortures of success," Kircher said. "Success in our business, the trade-union business, means getting workers to middle-class status. You succeed and *Huelga* is just going to be an exciting recollection. The guy who carried a banner in 1966—well, in five years you're going to have a hard time getting him to a union meeting. Revolutions become institutions, that's a truism of our business. Look at the *Marseillaise*. That used to be the rallying cry of the radicals. Now it's the song of state."

I did not share his optimism. The will of the Valley, if not its social fabric, is holding, and the threat of mechanization coupled with the prospect of a long tedious battle in the fields could in the end sap even the strength of *la causa*. As I left Delano that day, the scorched September leaves were just beginning to fall and the sun blazed down on the somnolent streets and on the horizonless fields that stretched away from either side of Highway 99. I could not help but think that it would be a long time before *Nosotros Venceremos* became the song of the Great Central Valley.

1971

It was a long time before I returned to Delano. I passed
it a number of times on my way to Sacramento, where I
have family, but I never had the urge to stop. It was not
a place of old friends and warm memories. It was a place
where I had been and a place I was glad to leave. There
was something sad and brooding about it, an endless, un-
finished chapter straddling Highway 99. I remembered
the last time I had been there. It was four years ago, in
March 1967, and I stopped only by accident. I was driving
from Sacramento to Los Angeles, that interminable drive,
like driving 400 miles on a pool table, comforted only by
the car radio and the Valley deejays' version of hard rock
—a little Burt Bacharach, a touch of the Fifth Dimension.
There was no traffic, the speedometer needle kept inching
up. I had no intention of stopping in Delano, but just
outside the city limits, I noticed that I needed gas. As I
cruised onto the freeway off-ramp, I noticed the blinking
red light of the Highway Patrol.

The officer was very young, twenty-two at the outside,
with one of those OCS haircuts, all skin on the sides, a
part and two inches on the top. He was wearing smoked
sunglasses and a lot of Mennen's Skin Bracer. He was very
courteous.

"You were going 85 mph in a 70 mph zone," the Highway Patrolman said.

There was no argument. I sat in the front seat of his patrol car and gave him my driver's license. He asked my occupation. I told him. He put his pen down.

"You know about this grape strike here? That's a good story."

I told him I was in the process of writing it. For what magazine, he wanted to know. He was interested now. He had inserted the carbon paper, but still had not made a mark on the ticket. I told him the name of the magazine.

"Is that a liberal magazine or a conservative magazine?"

"They let you think pretty much what you want."

It seemed to satisfy him. He carefully put his pen back into his shirt pocket and closed the flap over it.

"You ever met this Cesar Chavez?"

"Yes."

He was closing his summons book. "He a Communist?"

"No."

The youth was silent for a moment. Then he unbuttoned his shirt flap and took out his pen. He reopened his summons book. "You were doing 85 mph in a 70 mph zone," he said.

In a sense, after four years, this brief encounter with the California Highway Patrol remains my most vivid impression of Delano. When asked "what was it like" or "what does it all mean," it is with difficulty that I can recall anything else. There are other things I remember, of course, but they are all equally tangential to what was happening. In no sense could they be used to make a point, to show a moral. I remember a cool night in the foothills of the Sierra when a panicky young farm worker was casually seduced by a California golden girl. I remember the boy still desperately picking on his guitar even as he was being led off to the bedroom and I remember that the next morning when the girl knocked on my door to wake me up she wasn't wearing any clothes. I remember a grower named Jack Pandol, whom I liked personally better than anyone I met in Delano, telling me that he really had very little in common with his brother-in-law, who was also a farmer, and when I asked why, he said simply, "He's in alfalfa. I'm in grapes."

I did not sense then, as I do now, the gulf between all I heard and read and saw—the "story"—and what strikes me now increasingly as the "real," those moments that have no function in the "story," but which seem in retrospect more interesting, more imaginatively to the point, more evocative of how we live and what we feel. Jack Pandol's story about his alfalfa-growing brother-in-law was real and said more about what it was like to be a grower than all the cant I heard and all the account books I read that hot summer. There was in it the sense of being alone, of embattlement, the feeling that if he didn't have much in common with his brother-in-law, he was going to have even less in common with Chavez. And the California golden girl's seduction of the young farm worker was real. It is clear to me now that no amount of good faith on her part could bridge the chasm of social and sexual custom between them. She worked hard and loyally for Chavez, but in the end I think she had even less communion with the *campesinos* than Pandol.

I think I became further estranged from the events in Delano by the promiscuity of the attention lavished on Chavez. The insatiable appetites of instant communication have necessitated a whole new set of media ground rules, predicated not only on the recording of fact but also on the projection of glamour and image and promise. The result of this cultural nymphomania is that we have become a nation of ten-minute celebrities. People, issues and causes hit the charts like rock groups, and with approximately as much staying power. For all the wrong reasons, Chavez had all the right credentials—mysticism, non-violence, the nobility of the soil. But distastefully implicit in instant apotheosis is the notion of causes lost; saints generally fail and when they do not, the constant scrutiny of public attention causes a certain moral devaluation. Enthusiasm for a cause is generally in inverse proportion to actually becoming involved. One could fete grape workers, as the rich and beautiful once did on a Long Island estate, without thinking about, if indeed one even knew about, the Suffolk County potato workers only a few miles away living in conditions equally as wretched as any pickers in the Great Central Valley of California.

And so I followed the strike from afar. Desultorily I kept a file, neatly packaging the headlines in a series of folders. *Note & file:* Chavez boycotts table grapes nationally; *cross-reference:* Lindsay administration halts purchase of grapes by New York city institutions; *cross-reference:* Pentagon increases grape purchases to help growers. *Note & file:* Chavez embarks on a penitential fast; *cross-reference:* Robert Kennedy takes communion with Chavez as fast ends; *cross-reference:* Robert Kennedy and Cesar Chavez—who stands to gain the most? *Note & file:* 1969—large crop, depressed prices, boycott; *cross-reference:* strike speeds automation. *Note & file:* 1970—short crop, recession, boycott. *Note & file:* July 29, 1970—Delano growers capitulate, sign three-year contract with Chavez. "We are happy peace has come to this Valley," says a growers' spokesman. "It has been a mutual victory."

"Mutual victory"—the phrase had the hollow sound of rhetoric and too often the territory behind rhetoric is mined with equivocation. I wondered who, if anyone, really was victorious in Delano, wondered if victory was tinctured with ambiguity. And so for the first time in four years I returned to Delano, goaded there by the instinctive feeling that there are no solutions, only at best amelioration, and never ultimate answers, final truths.

> *I've never talked to Cesar Chavez. But you know, I've been around longer than he has and I think I know these people better than he does. Maybe he'd learn something if he talked to me.*
>
> Former U.S. Senator George Murphy (R., Cal.), May 1969

It was Robert Kennedy who legitimized Chavez. Prior to 1966, when the U.S. Senate Subcommittee on Migratory Labor held hearings in the Valley, no Democrat would touch the Chavez movement. It had always been necessary to attract a few Southern votes in order for pro-labor legislation to pass in the Congress, and Southern agrarians would not toss a bone toward labor unless farm workers were excluded from all provisions of any proposed bill. Robert Kennedy was no stranger either to expedience or to good politics and, along with most of organized labor, saw little to be gained by an identification with Chavez. But he was persuaded to attend the hearings in March 1966 by one of his aides, Peter Edelman, acting in concert with a handful of union officials alive to the drama in

Delano. Even while flying to California, Kennedy was reluctant to get involved, demanding of his staff, "Why am I going?" He finally showed up at the hearings a day late. The effect was electric, a perfect meeting of complementary mystiques. Kennedy—ruthless, arrogant, a predator in the corridors of power. And Chavez—nonviolent, Christian, mystical, not without a moral imperative of his own.

For the next two years, it was almost impossible to think of Chavez except in conjunction with Robert Kennedy. The Kennedys sponged up ideas, and implicit in Chavez was the inexorable strength of an idea whose time had come. Kennedy's real concern for the farm workers helped soften his image as a self-serving keeper of his brother's flame and in turn plugged Chavez into the power outlets of Washington and New York. For the first time Chavez became fashionable, a national figure registering on the nation's moral thermometer. Robert Kennedy and Cesar Chavez—the names seemed wired into the same circuitry, the one a spokesman, the other a symbol for the constituency of the dispossessed.

Whatever the readings on fame's Geiger counter, it was a bad time in Delano. The strike, in 1968, was mired in quicksand. An attempt to organize the grape ranches of the Coachella Valley had failed miserably. The threat of violence hung heavy. A newspaper in Indio reported a $10,000 bounty on Chavez's head. However unsubstantiated the rumor, bounty spelled contract, and contract spelled hit. Bodyguards dogged Chavez's footsteps and a German shepherd watchdog patrolled his door. And then Robert Kennedy was killed the same day that Chavez had dispatched platoons into the barrios of East Los

Angeles to round up votes for his benefactor in the California Democratic primary. Chavez showed up at Kennedy's funeral at St. Patrick's Cathedral in New York characteristically late, dressed in a sweater. He marched to an empty pew and stood throughout the ceremony, to the mounting annoyance of a group of U.S. Senators whose view he was blocking.

The strike had begun to lose its momentum the year before. Perelli-Minetti was the last Delano grower to sign with Chavez, and even that was by default. The grower had originally settled with the Teamsters, an agreement bitterly assailed by Chavez as a sweetheart contract, and it was only after the two unions had arbitrated their jurisdictions that UFWOC inherited the Perelli-Minetti workers. Chavez's next target was the Giumarra Vineyards, the largest table-grape growers in America, themselves controlling 10 percent of the annual crop. His strategy was a San Joaquin Valley version of the domino theory: knock over Giumarra and the other growers had to fall in line. But the Giumarras were a rough bunch of boys, a network of Sicilian fathers and brothers and sons and sons-in-law not especially known for their enlightened views about the labor movement. Even their lawyer was one of their own, John Giumarra, Jr., then not thirty, a Stanford Law School graduate who gave up an Orange County law practice to come home as the family's counsel and spokesman.

The strike against Giumarra proved one thing—there wasn't a picket line in the world that could force a grower to agree to a contract. It was next to impossible to certify a strike. Workers who were pulled out were readily replaced by scabs and green-carders—foreign nationals (in this case Mexicans) with U.S. work permits, or green cards. The pickers were usually out of town working at another farm before the applicable state agencies even arrived to verify their departure. Though green-carders were legally enjoined against working in a strike situation, they were free to work if no strike had been certified. And in the conflicting claims as to the number of workers who actually walked out at a struck farm, I am inclined for one reason to lean more toward the grower's figure than the union's: it simply defied all logic for a picker to go out on strike. However grandiose (by grower standards) a picker's hourly wage, his annual income was barely at subsistence level, if indeed that high. Given that picking is one of the most miserable jobs known to man, it is usually —for whatever social or cultural reasons—the best a picker can hold. So no matter how much he favored the union, he would have had to be a sainted fanatic to go on strike and further heighten both his own and his family's level of misery.

Against Giumarra, Chavez needed another edge and he fell back on the boycott he had used so successfully against Schenley and Di Giorgio. Both these concerns were public corporations, however, susceptible to stockholder pressure, and both had a line of consumer products that could be successfully boycotted. Table grapes were another thing altogether. There was no label identification; a bunch of grapes was a bunch of grapes. The problem did not seem to deter Chavez. He seems to regard a boycott almost as a religious experience. "It's like quicksand," he says. "It's irreversible. Once it gets going, it creates a life of its own. It reaches a point where nothing can stop it. It's like trying to fight the wind."

The Giumarras were equal to the blow. When UFWOC prevailed on stores to stop buying the Giumarra label, the firm began borrowing labels from other growers and using them in place of its own. Even a rebuke from the Food and Drug Administration charging that label switching was contrary to federal regulations did not deter the grower. By the end of 1967, Giumarra was using, by union count, 105 different labels. In retaliation, UFWOC early in 1968 extended its boycott beyond Giumarra to include every California grower of table grapes.

As the growers dug in, there was within the union a certain impatience, a certain fraying of the precepts of non-violence. The imperceptible erosion of the growers' position was not particularly heady to union militants steeped in the literature of the headlines, the combat communiqués from the core cities. There was a new truculence in the air; packing crates were burned, tires slashed, scabs roughed up. Chavez was not unaware of the nascent violence. Late in February 1968, he quietly began a penitential fast to redirect the movement back onto its non-violent course. Only on the sixth day of the fast did he alert aides to what he was doing. No one had to be apprised of its exploitative potential. The circus aspect of the next seventeen days (the fast lasted twenty-three days) dismayed a number of Chavez's stanchest supporters, who, while not doubting his intentions, nevertheless deplored the manner in which union aides pandered to the media that flocked to Delano. If not actively choreographing the fast, UFWOC officials did little to discourage the faithful who seemed to equate it with the Second Coming. Tents were pitched for farm workers maintaining a vigil for Chavez, and old women crawled on their knees from the highway to the quarters where he was lodged for the duration of the fast.

Whatever its indulgences, the fast was like a hypodermic full of pure adrenalin pumped into the union. It seemed to find new resolve, new strength. But the fast had also endangered Chavez's always perilous health. One of his legs is shorter than the other, one side of his pelvis smaller. Six months after his fast, his energies depleted, Chavez was hospitalized. His condition was diagnosed as a degenerating spinal disc. For months he remained virtually an invalid, resisting treatment. Then early in 1969, Senator Edward Kennedy, at his own expense, sent Dr. Janet Travell, the back specialist who had treated John Kennedy, to Delano to look at Chavez. Dr. Travell concluded that Chavez's problem was not spinal but the result of muscular breakdown in his back. Her treatment (among other things, she prescribed a rocking chair) gradually freed Chavez from his bed. Without pain for the first time in nearly a dozen years, he could turn his full attention to a strike that by mid-1969 seemed endless.

In John Giumarra, Jr., the growers had their most impressive spokesman. In contrast to the primitives of the elder generation, he seemed practically epicene. Not for him any vulgar Red-baiting; even the ritualistic evocation of outside agitation was toned down. The 1968 election gave the growers a friendly administration in Washington, and an almost immediate by-product was a substantial jump in the Pentagon's purchase of table grapes. Pentagon spokesmen indignantly denied that the increased purchases were meant to undercut the boycott, claiming instead that military *chefs de cuisine* had merely whipped up a number of new grape delicacies. The growers even developed a degree of media sophistication of their own. The California Table Grape Growers Association hired J. Walter Thompson, the nation's largest advertising agency, to come up with a campaign extolling table grapes (it seemed impossible for a while to pick up a service magazine without the eyes feasting on some alchemy of grapes and sour cream and brown sugar) and also engaged Whitaker & Baxter, a public-relations firm specializing in political causes (it handled the American Medical Association's effort against Medicare), to produce material countering the boycott. The gist of this campaign was that Chavez was being kept alive not so much by fuzzy-minded urban liberals boycotting grapes as by the greed of the AFL-CIO. Organized labor, according to this argument, had developed with age a severe case of varicose veins. While union membership continues to increase, the percentage of the population it represents decreases; there are fewer blue-collar workers, while white-collar workers are difficult to organize. Therefore the attraction of the nation's two million farmworkers. UFWOC's dues are $3.50 a month, $7,000,000 a month if all two million workers are organized, $84,000,000 a year in the coffers of the AFL-CIO.

The beauty of such an argument is that innuendo does the work. But beyond the rhetoric, the growers were hurting. In New York, the world's largest market for table grapes, the boycott had cut the number of railroad boxcars unloaded in 1968 by a third; in Baltimore by nearly half. Many supermarket chains simply refused to carry California table grapes. In some instances, their motives were not altogether humanitarian. Union locals hinted broadly that, unless grapes came out of the stores, butchers and retail clerks would not cross UFWOC picket lines. Not long after the NLRB put a stop to such intimidation, fires were discovered in at least three New York A & Ps, cause in each instance unknown, although it was the considered opinion of the city's chief fire marshall that the boycott might have been a contributing factor. If a message was intended, it was received loud and clear. Across the country, grapes disappeared from the shelves.

The success of the boycott was enhanced by the uncertain state of the economy. Agriculture is a carnivorous business. Farmers feed on the misfortunes of their own; a disastrous frost in Arizona profits the growers of the same crop in the San Joaquin Valley. Crops are subject to rollercoaster fluctuations. The large harvest in 1969 depressed grape prices; the short crop in 1970 was more susceptible to strike and boycott. What the Nixon economists called a "seasonal adjustment" was a full-fledged recession and it was bleeding growers as it bled the rest of the country. The grape business was plagued by bankruptcies. Money was short, interest was high. Farmers were paying 9 and 10 percent for bank loans to start their crop; the shakier the grower's finances, the higher interest he had to pay.

His predicament, however, was not designed to elicit much sympathy. Though growers might claim that they were getting stuck with someone else's check, the bill for a hundred years of often malevolent paternalism was now being called in. If that bill seemed inflated by a surcharge of moral indignation, one had only to remember how long past due it was. The growers had finally run afoul of the times. Halfway around the world, the nation was involved in a hated, pernicious war. It was a house divided, doubting itself, forced to examine charges that it was racist both at home and abroad. It was difficult to conjure up a charismatic grower; the words just did not adhere. A man with thousands of acres worth millions of dollars simply did not have the emotional appeal of a faceless crowd of brown-skinned men, women and children eking out a fetid existence, crammed into substandard housing, isolated by language and custom from the rest of a community that scorned them. Never mind that the grower was mortgaged to the eyeballs, strangling on 9 and 10 percent interest payments. In the summer of 1970, high interest rates did not sing like food stamps.

The first break came from a handful of growers in the Coachella Valley. They signed with UFWOC and boxes of their grapes, adorned with the union's black-eagle emblem, were exempted from the boycott. After the May harvest, the union growers found their grapes bringing 25¢ to $1 more per box than those of the boycotted farmers. The lesson was not lost on the Delano growers. Late one night in July, John Giumarra, Jr., made his move. From a pay telephone at a dance he was attending in Bakersfield, he called Jerome Cohen, UFWOC's lawyer, in Delano. He told Cohen that he was flying out of Bakersfield at nine the next morning on a mission that could have "drastic consequences" for the grape industry; he asked if he could meet with Chavez before he made this "major move." (He did not mention what this major move was, and when I asked him six months later, he still refused. "It's water under the bridge," Giumarra said.) Cohen got hold of Chavez, who had been making a speech that night in San Rafael. Tired though he was, Chavez agreed to an immediate meeting. At 2 a.m., the parties met at the Stardust Motel in Delano and negotiated for the next six hours. Early Sunday morning they had reached tentative agreement. That same day Giumarra presented the agreement to the other Delano growers. I asked him how they had reacted. "Well, we had already stuck our foot in the water and I guess they thought it wouldn't hurt to see where negotiations led," Giumarra recalled. "But I wouldn't say any of the growers jumped up and down and said, 'Gee, hand me a contract.'"

Three days later, the twenty-six Delano growers signed a contract with UFWOC. The agreement called for $1.80 an hour, plus 20¢ per box incentive pay the first year, escalating to $2.10 an hour the third. Outwardly there was a sense of collective relief that after five years hostilities had ended. But there were still some residual hard feelings. Most centered around the stipulation that Chavez would supply every worker from a union hiring hall. Privately there was not a grower in Delano who thought UFWOC could deliver a full crew in time for the harvest. (The question was academic that first summer, as the harvest was already underway when the contract was signed and growers had full crews in the fields.) If UFWOC has not supplied enough workers by the start of the harvest, the contract allows growers to hire pickers on their own. But farmers fear that if they are forced to wait that long, their crops might start to rot. I asked John Giumarra, Jr., what action he would take in this eventuality.

"I'll burn your book," he replied without hesitation.

That was the end of the grape strike. The lettuce strike

in Salinas had already begun. Even as the conflict in Delano was winding down, Chavez had informed the lettuce growers in the Salinas Valley that he wished to organize their field workers. With almost indecent haste, the Salinas growers responded by soliciting the Teamsters, and twenty-four hours before the Delano contract was signed, they announced an agreement allowing the Teamsters to represent their field hands. Whatever the Teamsters were, what they were not was a union run by a radical Mexican mystic, and to the growers this was a most seductive enticement.

Since Chavez and the Teamsters had agreed three years before not to poach on each other's territory, the Salinas announcement was tantamount to a declaration of war. Late in August, Chavez struck the Salinas ranches. On the first day of the strike, between five and seven thousand workers walked off the job. The mood at UFWOC was euphoric. Never before had Chavez been able to pull workers out of the fields in any substantial numbers. The effect on the growers was immediate. Railroad carloads of lettuce shipped out of Salinas slipped from a normal 250 a day to as low as 35. In some areas the wholesale price of lettuce soared from $1.75 a crate to $6; in Los Angeles supermarkets the retail price rose 10¢ a head in a single day. Grower losses mounted to $500,000 a day. The numbers were enough to convince a few of the larger Salinas growers to sign with UFWOC. "The Teamsters had our contract," said a spokesman for Inter-Harvest, a subsidiary of United Fruit, "but UFWOC had our workers."

The majority of Salinas growers did not see it that way. In vain they tried to get an injunction against the strike, claiming they were the victims of a jurisdictional dispute between UFWOC and the Teamsters; a judge in Santa Maria ruled against the injunction on the grounds that there was insufficient evidence that the Teamsters actually had the support of the field workers. The Teamsters seemed to be schizophrenic about the whole thing. On the one hand, Teamster antipathy toward Chavez and his "smelly hippies" had long been documented; on the other, the Teamsters could count. The Teamster solution was to renege on its contracts with the growers and turn them over to UFWOC. The growers would have none of it; a marriage of convenience was still a marriage. It was an unprecedented situation—management holding to the sanctity of contracts for workers the union no longer wanted to represent. Not quite sure what to do, the Teamsters bent a few UFWOC skulls to keep in practice and talked a lot about law and order. Nor did the uncompromising majesty of the law make it seem any less droll. Less than three weeks after the Santa Maria decision, a judge in Salinas, ruling on virtually the same evidence, issued a permanent injunction against all UFWOC strike activity in the Salinas area.

Chavez's response was immediate. Hardly were his picket lines withdrawn than he ordered a nationwide boycott of all non-UFWOC lettuce in California and Arizona. Almost predictably hewing to the script of Delano, the first two growers to yield, Freshpict and Pic 'N Pac, were both subsidiaries of large consumer corporations (Purex and S. S. Pierce) concerned that a boycott might spread to their more visible packaged products on supermarket shelves. The other Salinas growers had no such concerns and, except for one defection, stood firm. In Salinas's least dreary restaurant, Caesar Salad was renamed Salinas Valley Salad (it was an affront to the palate under any name). Ironically, Chavez's most prominent foe in Salinas, Bud Antle, Inc., was not really a particular UFWOC target. In a situation almost unique in California, Bud Antle's lettuce workers had been under union contract since 1961. Not that Bud Antle's intentions in allowing the organization of their field workers were entirely altruistic. Nine years before, the Teamsters had lent the financially straitened company $1,000,000 and the *quid pro quo* was a union contract for, among others, the lettuce workers. Though he frequently alluded to the Teamster loan, Chavez had no real wish to challenge the contract. But in an across-the-board boycott, things get broken; it was the classic case of the omelet and the egg.

The boycott against Bud Antle landed Chavez in jail for the first time in his organizing career. Under court injunction to end the boycott against the firm, Chavez refused. Three weeks before Christmas 1970, a Salinas judge ordered him into jail until he did so. However impeccable the court order legally, the jailing of Chavez backfired against the growers emotionally. In plain terms, the lettuce boycott had been up to this point a flop. Five grinding years of strike and boycott against the grape growers had simply run down the batteries of Chavez's supporters. His incarceration, however, was an instant recharge. A vigil was set up outside the Salinas County jail. The star names pilgrimaged to Salinas, led by the widows Coretta King and Ethel Kennedy, whose very presence was a stark reminder of those insane few months in 1968 when martyrdom seemed the only resolution to the nation's problems. On Christmas Eve, Chavez was released from jail pending a hearing on his case by a higher tribunal. But his jailing had given the boycott so much momentum that the Teamsters announced a boycott of their own, a boycott against the loading or unloading of any UFWOC-picked crops, at least until UFWOC called off its campaign against Bud Antle. The permutations seemed limitless. It was as if the lessons of Delano were written on the wind.

FACTS:

There are 5 million Mexican-Americans in the United States. They are the nation's second largest minority. Almost 90 percent live in the five southwestern states of Arizona, California, Colorado, New Mexico and Texas. They comprise 15 percent of the population of Texas, 10 percent of the population of California and 28 percent of the population of New Mexico. More than one-third live in "official" poverty on incomes of less than $3,000 a year. Their birth rate is twice the national average, and the mortality rate for infants less than a year old is twice that of Anglos. Their median age is eleven years less than that of the Anglo; 42 percent of the Mexican-American population is under the age of fifteen. They average approximately eight years of schooling, four years fewer than the Anglos. Half of all Mexican-Americans who enter high school drop out before finishing. The Mexican-American unemployment rate is twice that of Anglos, and almost 80 percent work at unskilled or semi-skilled jobs.

The harvest from the grape strike is like a short crop in a good year. Because of Chavez and Chavez alone, it is now possible to predict that all farm labor will be organized in the foreseeable future. Perhaps not by UFWOC. Old habits die hard, and for growers a farm union is hard enough to swallow without Chavez as a chaser. Most would cheerfully sign their workers over to something like the International Ladies Garment Workers Union if they thought it was the only way to thwart him. Even grower associations are now calling for farm labor to come under the umbrella of the National Labor Relations Board, and the sound of their platitudes is heard in the land: "It is time that farm workers be allowed to join the 1970s. Too long have they been cut off from the mainstream of the American labor movement." (Applause.) Six years ago this might have been enough to buy off a strike. Not now. Success has made Chavez very sophisticated and he is in no hurry to embrace the NLRB. As amended by the Taft-Hartley and Landrum-Griffin acts, the NLRB now prohibits the two major weapons in Chavez's arsenal—secondary boycotts and organizational strikes. He is very much aware that since the passage of these two amendments no large group of unskilled labor has been organized. Until adjustments can be made, inclusion under the NLRB is a lollipop Chavez would just as soon forswear.

And yet beyond UFWOC's demonstrable success, beyond its cool reading of the times, there is little room for euphoria. The nagging thought persists that the strike in Delano was irrelevant except as an abstraction. Victory there was like administering sedatives to a terminal-cancer patient, a mercy, a kindness, death-easing rather than life-saving, a victory finally important less for its fulfilled intentions than for what, unintended, it presaged. Higher wages, a fund of new members, greater independence from management—these traditional benchmarks of labor

achievement do not really apply to Delano. In the narrow-
est sense, a union of farm workers can only lighten its
members' burden of misery. The figures are simply too
relentless. Nearly 700,000 workers earned wages in California's fields and vineyards in 1967 (the most recent
year for which comprehensive statistics are available),
and while they earned $1.78 an hour on the farm, their
average annual income for *all* work, both farm and non-
farm, was only $1,709. And though the 700,000 included
foremen, crew leaders, supervisors and other year-round
employees, only 31,000 earned as much as $5,000 that year
in farm work.

There is simply too little future in farm work. While
farms grow bigger and productivity increases, the number
of farm workers steadily declines. Four percent of California's growers own nearly 70 percent of the farm land;
8 percent hire over 70 percent of the farm labor. Over the
past twenty-five years, the number of farms in California
has been cut by more than half. Cities roll past the suburbs
into the country, swallowing up small farms that histor-
ically soaked up the glut in the labor market, farms far
more valuable to the grower as subdivisions than they
ever were as raw acreage. Two years ago, less than 2 percent of the wine grapes in Fresno County were harvested
by machine; the estimate for 1971 is more than 30 percent.
In three years the Fresno County Economic Opportunities
Commission predicts that 65 percent of the wine and
raisin grapes in the San Joaquin Valley will be picked
mechanically. Even table grapes could be picked auto-
matically were consumers willing to buy them in boxes,
like strawberries, instead of insisting on the aesthetic
appeal of bunches. It is estimated that mechanical pickers

will cost Fresno County farm workers nearly $2 million in wages during 1971 and that by 1973 some 4,500 heads of families will be displaced by machines.

Growers recite these figures as if they were graven on stone. There is little doubt that Chavez has speeded up the wheels of automation, but the implication is that no one ever dreamed of it until he came along; indeed that, were it not for Chavez, no machine ever developed, no matter how economical, could ever separate a grower from his beloved workers. Engagingly enough, the growers really believe it.

The curious thing about Cesar Chavez is that he is as little understood by those who would canonize him as by those who would condemn him. To the saint-makers, Chavez seemed the perfect candidate. His crusade was devoid of the ambiguities of urban conflict. With the farm workers there were no nagging worries about the mugging down the block, the rape across the street, the car boosted in front of the house. It was a cause populated by simple Mexican peasants with noble agrarian ideas, not by surly unemployables with low IQs and Molotov cocktails.

All that is missing in this fancy is any apprehension of where the real importance of Cesar Chavez lies. The saintly virtues he had aplenty; it is doubtful that the media would have been attracted to him were it not for those virtues, and without the attention of the media the strike could not have survived. But Chavez also had the virtues of the labor leader, less applauded publicly perhaps, but no less admirable in the rough going—a will of iron, a certain deviousness, an ability to hang tough in the clinches. Together these twin disciplines kept what often seemed a hopeless struggle alive for six years, six years that kindled an idea that made the idealized nuances of Delano pale by comparison.

For the ultimate impact of Delano will be felt not so much on the farm as in the city. In the vineyards, Chavez fertilized an ethnic and cultural pride ungerminated for generations, but it was in the barrio that this new sense of racial identity flourished as if in a hothouse. Once four-fifths of the Mexican-American population lived in the rural outback, but as the farm worker became a techno-logical as well as a social victim, his young deserted the hoe for the car wash. Today that same four-fifths float through the urban barrio like travelers without passports, politically impoverished, spiritually disenfranchised. State and municipal governments have so carefully charted the electoral maps that it is impossible for a Mexican-Amer-ican to get elected without Anglo sufferance. California's only Mexican-American congressman depends on Anglo suburbs for more than half his support and in the state legislature the gerrymandering is even more effective; there was in 1971 only one Mexican assemblyman and no state senator. It was a system that placed high premium on the Tio Taco, or Uncle Tom.

But since Delano there is an impatience in the barrio with old formulas and old deals and old alliances, a dis-satisfaction with a diet of crumbs, a mood—more than surly, if not yet militant—undermining and finally begin-ning to crack the ghetto's historic inertia. Drive down Whittier Boulevard in East Los Angeles, a slum in the Southern California manner, street after street of tiny bungalows and parched lawns and old cars, a grid of mo-notony. The signs are unnoticed at first, catching the eye only after the second or third sighting, whitewashed on fences and abandoned storefronts, the paint splattered and uneven, signs painted on the run in the dark of night, "*Es mejor morir de pie que vivir de rodillas*"—"Better to die standing than live on your knees." The words are those of Emiliano Zapata, but the spirit that wrote them there was fired by Cesar Chavez.

It is with the young that the new mood is most prevalent. On the streets they sell orange posters that say nothing more than "*La Raza.*" At Lincoln High School in East Los Angeles, students walked out on strike as a protest against overcrowding and neglect, a strike that challenged the passivity of their elders as much as it did the apathy of the Anglo community. Go to any protest meeting in East Los Angeles and the doors are guarded by an indigenous force of young vigilantes called the Brown Berets. ("We needed a gimmick, we needed a name," one of their leaders told a reporter from *Time*. "We thought of calling ourselves the Young Citizens for Community Action, but that didn't sound right. We tried Young Chicanos, but that didn't work either. We thought of wearing big sombreros, but we figured people would just laugh at us. So we hit on the beret and someone said, 'Why not the Brown Berets?' And it clicked with all of us.")

The pride that Chavez helped awaken took on a different tone in the barrio than in the vineyards. The farm workers' movement was essentially non-violent, an effort based on keeping and exhibiting the moral advantage. But in East Los Angeles today the tendency is to pick up life's lessons less from Gandhi than from the blacks. Traditionally, brown and black have been hostile, each grappling for that single spot on the bottom rung of the social

ladder. To the Mexican-American the Anglo world held
out the bangle of assimilation, a bribe to the few that kept
the many docile. Denied to blacks, assimilation for years
robbed the Chicano community of a nucleus of leadership. Today the forfeiture of this newly acquired cultural
awareness seems to the young Chicano a prohibitive price
to pay. The new courses in social bribery are taught by
the blacks.

What the barrio is learning from the blacks is the political sex appeal of violence. Three times in the past year,
East Los Angeles has erupted. The body count is still low,
less than the fingers on one hand, hardly enough to merit
a headline outside Los Angeles County. The official riposte
is a call for more law and order. The charges of police
brutality clash with the accusations of outside agitation.
But beyond the rhetoric there is new attention focused on
the ghetto. The vocabulary of the dispossessed is threat
and riot, the Esperanto of a crisis-reacting society, italicizing the poverty and discrimination and social deprivation in a way that no funded study or government commission ever could.

Like Malcolm X and Martin Luther King, Cesar Chavez
stands astride history less for what he accomplished than
for what he is. Like them, he has forged "in the smithy of
his soul," in Joyce's phrase, the "uncreated consciousness"
of a people. He is the manifestation of *la raza*, less the saint
his admirers make him out to be than a moral obsessive,
drilling into the decay of a system that has become a mor-
tuary of hopes. We are a nation with a notoriously short
attention span, needing saints but building into them a
planned obsolescence. The man who survives this curse of
instant apotheosis becomes like Cesar Chavez acutely

uncomfortable to have around, a visionary ever demanding our enlistment as he tries to force the stronghold of forgotten possibilities. He demands only that we be better. It is a simple demand, and a terrifying one.

There is something exquisite about rural California in January. It is the month of the rains, a clear, cold, almost refrigerated rain, invigorating as an amphetamine. The hills are so green they seem carpeted in Astroturf. Peacocks preen by the side of the road. The wail of a train whistle, almost unheard since childhood, pierces the Valley. In Delano there was a semblance of peace. On Main Street the bumper stickers that once said "Boycott Grapes" or "Buy California Grapes" were faded and peeling, like scar tissue from a fight everyone said they wished to forget. Out past the Voice of America transmitters on the Garces Highway, hard by the municipal dump, UFWOC has a new headquarters complex called Forty Acres. There is a gas station and an office and miscellaneous dilapidated buildings. What struck me most was how quiet it was. Underneath that vast empty sky at Forty Acres, even the lettuce strike was discussed with as little fervor as the weather. It was as if after five years of continuous combat everyone had come down with an attack of rhetorical laryngitis. Downtown there is talk of diversification, of attracting industry to Delano, of an industrial park. I was told about the labor pool—20 percent unemployment in the winter—and how a one-crop town needs to get into other things. The Chamber of Commerce and the city council have established the Delano Economic Expansion Project (DEEP) to lure industry into the area and hired the former manager of the Hanford (California) Chamber of Commerce to head it up. "One thing Cesar Chavez did for us," he says. "In Hanford I spent a whole lot of time trying to get people to know where Hanford is. In Delano I haven't had to do that." There was one other thing I noticed in Delano. I didn't know if it was a DEEP project or not. The sign on the outskirts of town used to say, "Hungry? Tired? Car Trouble? Need Gas? Stop in Delano." There is a new sign now out on Highway 99. It says, "DELANO. WELCOME ANY-TIME."